Air Fryer Dessert Recipes

100 Simple & Delicious Air Fryer Dessert Recipes

By

APRIL KELSEY

Air Fryer Dessert Recipes

Copyright © 2024 April Kelsey

All rights reserved.

ISBN: 9798863396194

COPYRIGHT © 2024

This book is protected by copyright. Any reproduction, storage, or transmission, whether electronic, mechanical, photocopying, recording, scanning, or otherwise, requires prior written permission from the publisher.

DISCLAIMER

All the material contained in this book is provided for educational and informational purposes only. No responsibility can be taken for any results or outcomes from using this material.

While every attempt has been made to provide accurate and practical information, the author does not assume any responsibility for the accuracy or use/misuse of this information.

ALL RIGHTS RESERVED. No part of this publication may be reproduced or transmitted in any form, electronic or mechanical, including photocopying, recording, or by any informational storage or retrieval system without express written, dated, and signed permission from the author.

Contents

Introduction 9
- How do air fryers work? 10
- Benefits of using an air fryer 11
- Understanding the Different Parts of an Air Fryer 12
- Safety Tips for Using an Air Fryer 13
- Foods that can be prepared in an air fryer 15
- Tips for air-frying success 17
- Maintenance and Care of Your Air Fryer 18
- Troubleshooting Common Issues with Air Fryers 19
- How to Use an Air Fryer 20

Recipes 22
- Air Fryer Chocolate Chip Cookies 22
- Air Fryer Brownies 26
- Air Fryer Apple Crisp 29
- Air Fryer Cinnamon Sugar Donuts 32
- Air Fryer Chocolate Cake 35
- Air Fryer Blueberry Muffins 38
- Air Fryer Banana Bread 41
- Air Fryer Carrot Cake 47
- Air Fryer S'mores 51
- Air Fryer Peanut Butter Cookies 54
- Air Fryer Chocolate-covered Strawberries 57
- Air Fryer Cinnamon Rolls 60
- Air Fryer Red Velvet Cake 63
- Air Fryer Peach Cobbler 66
- Air Fryer Pound Cake 69

Air Fryer Oreo Cheesecake 72

Air Fryer Nutella Brownies 75

Air Fryer Apple Pie 79

Air Fryer Bread Pudding 82

Air Fryer Pumpkin Pie 85

Air Fryer Chocolate Fudge 88

Air Fryer Chocolate Covered Pretzels 91

Air Fryer Rice Krispie Treats 94

Air Fryer Chocolate Croissants 97

Air Fryer Baked Apples 100

Air Fryer Lemon Pound Cake 103

Air Fryer Chocolate Donuts 106

Air Fryer Cinnamon Apple Chips 110

Air Fryer Blueberry Cobbler 112

Air Fryer Oatmeal Cookies 115

Air Fryer Peach Dumplings: 118

Air Fryer Sweet Potato Pie: 121

Air Fryer Caramel Apples 125

Air Fryer Chocolate Mousse: 128

Air Fryer Raspberry Cheesecake: 131

Air Fryer Churros 134

Air Fryer Almond Flour Chocolate Chip Cookies 138

Air Fryer Apple Cinnamon Cake: 141

Air Fryer Pop Tarts 144

Air Fryer Chocolate Covered Bananas 149

Air Fryer Zucchini Bread 152

Air Fryer Lemon Poppyseed Muffins 156

- Air Fryer Chocolate Brownie Cookies 159
- Air Fryer Blackberry Cobbler: 162
- Air Fryer Sweet Potato Fries with Maple Syrup 165
- Air Fryer Baked Peaches 168
- Air Fryer Blueberry Lemon Cake 171
- Air Fryer Chocolate Pudding 174
- Air Fryer Apple Cider Donuts 177
- Air Fryer Scones: 180
- Air Fryer Gingerbread Cookies: 183
- Air Fryer Caramelized Bananas: 186
- Air Fryer Apple Turnovers 188
- Air Fryer Oatmeal Raisin Cookies 191
- Air Fryer Mini Fruit Pies 194
- Air Fryer Coconut Macaroons 197
- Air Fryer Chocolate Hazelnut Cake 200
- Air Fryer Funnel Cake 203
- Air Fryer Pumpkin Spice Donuts 206
- Air Fryer Chocolate Caramel Brownies 209
- Air Fryer Mixed Berry Crisp 212
- Air Fryer Peanut Butter Fudge 215
- Air Fryer Sweet Potato Casserole 218
- Air Fryer Blueberry Lemon Bars 221
- Air Fryer Cinnamon Sugar Pretzels: 224
- Air Fryer Chocolate Covered Cherries: 226
- Air Fryer Strawberry Shortcake: 229
- Air Fryer Oreo Churros: 232
- Air Fryer Peach Hand Pies: 235

Air Fryer Caramel Popcorn 239
Air Fryer Lemon Ricotta Cake: 242
Air Fryer Blackberry Bread: 245
Air Fryer Chocolate Peanut Butter Cups: 248
Air Fryer Mini Cheesecakes: 251
Air Fryer Strawberry Jam Thumbprint Cookies: 254
Air Fryer Chocolate Chip Banana Bread: 256
Air Fryer Banana Foster: 259
Air Fryer Pumpkin Pie Bites: 262
Air Fryer Cinnamon Apple Fritters: 264
Air Fryer Chocolate Donuts: 266
Air Fryer Caramelized Pineapple 269
Air Fryer Maple Glazed Donut Holes 271
Air Fryer Lemon Curd Tartlets 274
Air Fryer Peach Melba: 277
Air Fryer Cherry Clafoutis 279
Air Fryer Chai Spiced Rice Pudding 281
Air Fryer Mixed Berry Galette: 283
Air Fryer Chocolate Soufflé: 286
Air Fryer Cinnamon Sugar Apple Rings 289
Air Fryer Peanut Butter and Jelly Donuts 292
Air Fryer Sweet Cornbread Muffins: 294
Air Fryer Apple Cinnamon Empanadas: 296
Air Fryer Lemon Pound Cake: 298
Air Fryer Chocolate Fondue: 301
Air Fryer Vanilla Bean Crème Brûlée 303
Air Fryer Blackberry Hand Pies: 305

Air Fryer Salted Caramel Popovers:	**308**
Air Fryer Cinnamon Bun Twists	**311**
Air Fryer Monkey Bread	**314**

Introduction

The invention of the air fryer changed the way food was prepared forever. These little gadgets have revolutionized cooking methods. The secret to an air fryer's success is its unique cooking method.

Unlike typical deep-frying, air fryers use little or no oil. This solution allows you to indulge in your favorite fried meals without worrying about counting calories or fat.

And no more messy oil! No pan scrubbing or grease clean up. Clean the air fryers inside with a moist towel, and you're ready.

Air fryers are remarkable kitchen gadgets that offer a multitude of benefits. The capability of an air fryer to cook a wide variety of food is one of this appliance's most impressive aspects. You can cook crispy chicken wings, roasted vegetables, and even desserts.

How do air fryers work?

The key to this process is the air fryer's heating element at the top of the appliance. When you turn on an air fryer, the heating source inside the machine heats the air inside the machine to a very high temperature. Usually between 300 and 400 degrees Fahrenheit. This superheated air is circulated through the food by a fan above the heating element.

The fan generates a hot air vortex that encircles the food and cooks it simultaneously. The hot air evaporates any moisture on the surface of the food, creating a golden-brown crust. This gives air-fried foods their crispy texture.

The fan also circulates hot air around the meal. It distributes heat to cook food. It's important since you don't have to flip or rotate the food. As with conventional frying.

Benefits of using an air fryer

Healthier Cooking: Air fryers need little or no oil. So you can fry your favorite things with less fat and fewer calories than you would normally.

Universal Cooking: Air fryers are not just for frying foods. They can be used for baking, roasting, grilling, and reheating meals. You can even make snacks and desserts as well.

Convenience: Air fryers are simple and need little cleaning after use, with lightning-fast cooking times. It's perfect for families on the go or anyone who values their time. Whip up tasty meals in no time with these must-have kitchen gadgets.

Saves Time and Energy: Air fryers save time in the kitchen. Moreover, they use less energy than traditional ovens. This may save energy and money.

Safe and Easy to Use: Air fryers are considered very safe. They come with safety features like auto shut-off and cool-touch handles.

They are also easy to use. Simple settings make it easy to set the time and temperature for cooking.

No Grease or Mess: Since air fryers need little or no oil, there is no grease or mess to clean up after cooking. They're great for cooking healthy meals without a lot of effort.

Great for Small Spaces: Air fryers are smaller than regular ovens and take up less counter space. So they are an excellent choice for tiny kitchens or flats.

Preserve Food Nutrients: Air fryers cook food quickly and at high temperatures. Unlike typical frying processes, they preserve food nutrients.

Understanding the Different Parts of an Air Fryer

An air fryer is made up of several essential parts, including:

- **Basket or Tray:** This is where you place your food. It's normally dishwasher-safe and removable.
- **Heating Element:** This produces heat that cooks the food in the basket or tray.
- **Fan:** The fan helps Air evenly distribute heat to the meal by circulating hot air around it.

- **Temperature Control:** This lets you set a food's cooking temperature.
- **Additional Features:** Some air fryers have a few other features, such as many cooking settings, timers, and automatic shut-off functions.

Safety Tips for Using an Air Fryer

Air fryers are safe, but safety precautions are still necessary. Here are air fryer safety tips:

- Read the manual before using your air fryer.
- Always stay with the air fryer while it is in use. This will help you prevent accidents and respond quickly in an emergency.
- Place the air fryer on a flat, stable, level, and firm surface so it does not accidentally topple over.
- Avoid placing the air fryer near water sources like sinks or taps. This increases the electric shock and appliance damage risk.
- Use the air fryer in a well-ventilated area. This prevents smoke and steam from setting off fire alarms or causing breathing problems.

- Avoid overcrowding the air fryer: Overcrowding the basket restricts and blocks airflow and causes uneven cooking. To cook food uniformly, cook in batches.
- Air fryers cook food without oil. But a few specific recipes need a little oil for taste or texture. When using oil, use the right amount as specified in the recipe.
- Do not touch the air fryer while it's operating. Avoid touching it, as it can get hot and cause burns. Remove food from the frying basket using oven gloves or tongs.
- Clean the air fryer regularly after each use.

Follow these safety tips to operate your air fryer safely and efficiently. Enjoy crispy, tasty meals without worrying!

Foods that can be prepared in an air fryer

Overview of the types of foods that can be cooked in an air fryer so you can start cooking up a storm

- **Vegetables:** Air fryers cook veggies without oil well. Roast or fry Brussels sprouts, broccoli, cauliflower, carrots, and sweet potatoes perfectly.
- **Meats:** Air fryers are perfect for cooking meat. Cook chicken wings, steak, hog chops, hamburgers, meatballs, sausages, etc. One full chicken in an air fryer
- **Seafood:** Seafood may be air-fried. The air fryer makes fish crispy and juicy. Air-frying shrimp, fish, and scallops is healthier than frying.
- **Frozen Foods:** Cook frozen chicken nuggets, mozzarella sticks, and French fries perfectly in an air fryer. They cook frozen foods quickly and evenly, giving you a crispy and delicious snack in no time.

- **Desserts:** Air fryers may prepare sweets too. Donuts, apple chips, and chocolate chip cookies may be made in an air fryer. An air fryer makes crunchy, gooey desserts.
- **Baked Goods:** You may also prepare baked items like cookies, bread, muffins, and cupcakes.
- **Snacks and Appetizers:** popcorn, onion rings, jalapeño poppers, potato skins, and more can be air-fried.

Tips for air-frying success

- **Preheat the Air Fryer:** Preheat your air fryer like an oven before cooking. This ensures consistent cooking and prevents food from sticking to the basket.
- **Don't Overcrowd the Basket:** If you need to cook a lot of food at once, it's best to cook it in batches or use a bigger air fryer.
- **Use a Light Coating of Oil:** A spray bottle or brush to apply the oil can help ensure even coverage.
- **Shake or Flip the Food During Cooking:** Shake or turn the basket throughout frying to minimize sticking and even cooking. It also crisps the food.
- **Experiment with Seasonings and Spices:** Air fryers are wonderful for experimenting with herbs and spices to increase food taste. Try different flavors to discover your favorites.
-

Maintenance and Care of Your Air Fryer

When cleaning and maintaining your air fryer, remember a few important steps. These include:

- **Cleaning the Basket or Tray:** The basket or tray is where you place your food when using the air fryer. So it's important to keep it clean. Most baskets and trays can be removed from the air fryer and washed in the sink with warm, soapy water. You can also place them in the dishwasher if they are dishwasher-safe.

- **Cleaning the Heating Element and Fan:** The heating element and fan can become coated with grease and food particles over time. It's reducing the efficiency of your air fryer. Remove debris from these areas using a gentle brush or cloth.

- **Wiping Down the Exterior:** The exterior of your air fryer can also collect grease and food particles. Clean it frequently using a moist towel.
- **Removing and Cleaning the Drip Tray:** The drip tray collects oil dripping off your food during cooking. Remove and clean this tray regularly to prevent build up.

Troubleshooting Common Issues with Air Fryers

- **The Air Fryer Won't Turn On:** If your air fryer doesn't turn on, check to ensure it's plugged in correctly. If so, unplug and restart the machine.
- **The food isn't cooking properly.** If your food isn't cooking evenly or taking longer than expected, Ensure you're filling the basket or tray appropriately.
- **The air fryer is emitting smoke.** Remove food particles and oil from the heating element and fan if your air fryer smokes. You can also reduce the cooking temperature or use a lower-smoke-point oil.
- **Food Sticking to the Basket or Tray:** Before adding food, lightly spray the basket or pan with cooking spray or oil to keep it from sticking. Shake or turn the basket to ensure the food cooks and doesn't stick. If the food still sticks, clean the basket or pan well or change the time and temperature of the cooking.

How to Use an Air Fryer

- **Preheat the Air Fryer:** It's always good to preheat before cooking. However, it is dependent on the dish you are preparing. You can preheat for 3–5 minutes at your desired temperature. If not, preheating food takes longer and may cook unevenly. Also, food may be less crispy if you don't preheat.
- **Load the Basket:** Ensure the food fits in the air fryer basket. If the basket is overcrowded, the food may cook unevenly and turn mushy.
- **Set the Time and Temperature:** Set the time and temperature for cooking.
- **Cook the food:** shake the basket if you want your food cooked evenly throughout.
- **Remove the food:** Remove the air fryer basket using oven gloves or tongs after cooking. Wait a few minutes before serving the food.
- **Clean the Air Fryer:** After usage, wipe the air fryer with a moist cloth or sponge. The basket and any accessories can usually be washed in the dishwasher.

Recipes

Air Fryer Chocolate Chip Cookies

- Preparation Time: 15 minutes
- Cooking Time: 10 minutes
- Serving Size: 4

Nutrition Facts (per serving):

- Calories: 420
- Fat: 25g
- Protein: 2g
- Fiber: 2g

Ingredients:

- All-purpose flour - 1 and 1/4 cups
- Baking soda: 1/2 tsp
- Salt - 1/2 tsp
- Unsalted butter - 1/2 cup
- Granulated sugar - 1/2 cup
- Brown sugar - 1/2 cup
- Large egg - 1
- Vanilla extract - 1 tsp
- Semi-sweet chocolate chips - 1 cup

Instructions:

- Put the air fryer into pre-heating mode and set the temperature to 325°F (165°C) for 5 minutes.
- Mix the baking soda, salt, and all-purpose flour in a mixing bowl.
- In another bowl, mix softened 2/4 of the unsalted butter, sugar, and brown sugar. (Make sure the butter is melted.)
- Using a wooden spoon or electric mixer, beat it until fluffy. This usually takes a few minutes.

- Keep mixing until the butter and sugar are thoroughly mixed and smooth.
- Now add the egg and vanilla essence and mix until well combined.
- Add flour to the wet mixture and mix well.
- Add the semi-sweet chocolate chunks with the rest of the batter. Mix everything well.
- Spread cookie dough evenly on a parchment-lined baking sheet with a cookie scoop.
- Place a baking sheet in the air fryer. Cook it for 10 minutes or until golden brown.
- After frying, let the cookies cool for a few minutes before serving.

Variations

- Add chopped nuts, like walnuts or pecans, to the cookie batter before baking to give it a crunchier texture.
- Instead of semi-sweet chocolate chips, use white, milk, or a mix.

- Sea salt on biscuits before baking adds sweetness and saltiness.
- Add one tablespoon of espresso powder to the mix if you want the cookie batter to have a robust coffee flavor.

Air Fryer Brownies

- Preparation Time: 15 minutes
- Cooking Time: 20 minutes
- Serving Size: 4

Nutrition Facts (per serving):

- Calories: 420
- Fat: 25g
- Protein: 6g
- Fiber: 2g

Ingredients:

- All-purpose flour - 3/4 cup
- Cocoa powder - 1/2 cup
- Baking powder - 1/2 tsp

- Salt - 1/4 tsp
- Granulated sugar - 3/4 cup
- Unsalted butter (melted) - 1/2 cup
- Large eggs - 2
- Vanilla extract - 1 tsp
- Chocolate chips - 1/2 cup

Instructions:

- Put the air fryer into preheating mode and set the temperature to 325°F (165°C) for 5 minutes.
- Mix the all-purpose flour, cocoa powder, salt, and baking powder in a bowl.
- Mix the granulated sugar and unsalted butter in a separate bowl and whisk until smooth.
- Add the eggs and vanilla essence, and give the mixture a good beating until it is silky smooth and creamy.
- Now Mix the dry and wet ingredients in a steady stream until everything is well mixed. Don't over mix it.
- Add the chocolate chips.

- Grease the 6-inch baking sheet and pour in the brownie batter.
- Place the baking pan in the air fryer basket and air fry for 20 minutes or until the top is set and a toothpick inserted in the middle comes out clean.
- Remove the brownies from the air fryer and let them cool for a few minutes before slicing and serving.

Variations

- Add chopped nuts, like walnuts or almonds, to the brownie batter for a crunchier texture.
- Add a flavorful twist to the standard brownie recipe by mixing one tablespoon of peanut butter or Nutella into the batter before baking.
- Before serving, put a dollop of ice cream or whipped cream on each brownie and top with a cherry.
- Add one teaspoon of instant espresso powder to the mix if you want the brownie batter to have a thick and robust coffee flavor.

Air Fryer Apple Crisp

- Preparation Time: 15 minutes
- Cooking Time: 20 minutes
- Serving Size: 4

Nutrition Facts (per serving):

- Calories: 240
- Fat: 10g
- Protein: 2g
- Fiber: 4g

Ingredients:

- Apples (peeled, cored, and sliced) - 4 cups
- Lemon juice - 1 tbsp
- All-purpose flour - 1/4 cup
- Brown sugar - 1/4 cup
- Ground cinnamon - 1 tsp
- Salt - 1/4 tsp
- Rolled oats - 1/2 cup
- Unsalted butter (melted) - 1/4 cup

Instructions:

- Put the air fryer into preheating mode and set the temperature to 350°F (175°C) for 5 minutes.
- Add some lemon juice to a mixing dish and toss the sliced apples. It helps apples avoid turning brown.
- Now Mix the all-purpose flour, brown sugar, ground cinnamon, rolled oats, and salt in a separate bowl.
- Add the melted unsalted butter to the dry ingredients and mix until thoroughly mixed.
- Arrange the apple slices in a baking dish suitable for air fryer use and grease it with butter.
- Over the cut apples, evenly distribute the crumb mixture.
- Put the baking dish in the basket of the air fryer, and cook it for about 20 minutes, or until the apples are cooked through and the surface is golden brown.
- Take the apple crisp out of the air fryer, and it will be ready to serve after it has cooled for a few minutes.

Variations:

- To increase the sweetness of the crumb combination, stir in one tablespoon of honey or maple syrup.
- Try substituting other fruits, like apricots or berries for the apples in this recipe for a taste that's all your own.
- For a crispier finish, add chopped nuts like walnuts or almonds.

Air Fryer Cinnamon Sugar Donuts

- Preparation Time: 10 minutes
- Cooking Time: 8 minutes
- Serving Size: 4

Nutrition Facts (per serving):

- Calories: 240
- Fat: 10g
- Protein: 4g
- Fiber: 1g

Ingredients:

- All-purpose flour - 1 cup

- Granulated sugar - 1/4 cup
- Baking powder - 1 tsp
- Ground cinnamon - 1/2 tsp
- Salt - 1/4 tsp
- Milk - 1/2 cup
- Large egg - 1
- Unsalted butter (melted) - 2 tbsp
- Vanilla extract - 1 tsp
- Cooking spray
- Cinnamon sugar mixture (for topping) - 1/4 cup granulated sugar and 1 teaspoon ground cinnamon

Instructions:

- Put the air fryer into preheating mode and set the temperature to 350°F (175°C) for 5 minutes.
- Mix the all-purpose flour, baking soda, sugar, cinnamon, and salt in a large bowl using a whisk.
- In a separate bowl, Mix the milk, egg, melted unsalted butter, and vanilla extract and whisk until smooth.
- Mix the dry and liquid parts until the batter is completely incorporated.
- Apply a bit of melted butter or cooking spray to the air fryer donut molds to lightly oil them. Spoon the

batter into each mold, leaving about two-thirds empty. Smooth the tops if needed.
- In the preheated air fryer basket, place full doughnut molds. This may require batching, depending on the size of your air fryer.
- Air fryer for 8 minutes or until they have a golden brown color and are thoroughly cooked.
- Remove the donuts from the air fryer, coat them with cinnamon sugar mixture, and toss them until the doughnuts are completely covered.
- Enjoy while it's still fresh!

Variations:

- You can add melted chocolate or caramel sauce drizzled on top of them.
- To experiment with different flavors, replace the powdered cinnamon with ground nutmeg or cardamom.
- Served alongside sweetened cream or vanilla ice cream.

Air Fryer Chocolate Cake

- Preparation Time: 10 minutes
- Cooking Time: 18-20 minutes
- Serving Size: 4

Nutrition Facts (per serving):

- Calories: 420
- Fat: 20g
- Protein: 5g
- Fiber: 3g

Ingredients:

- All-purpose flour - 1 cup
- Granulated sugar - 1 cup
- Unsweetened cocoa powder - 1/2 cup
- Baking powder - 1 tsp
- Salt - 1/4 tsp
- Large egg - 1
- Milk - 1/2 cup
- Vegetable oil - 1/2 cup
- Vanilla extract - 1 tsp
- Cooking spray
- Powdered sugar (for topping)

Instructions:

- Put the air fryer into preheating mode and set the temperature to 330°F (165°C) for 5 minutes.
- Mix the all-purpose flour, granulated sugar, unsweetened baking powder, cocoa powder, and salt in a bowl using a whisk.
- In a separate mixing dish, combine the egg, milk, vegetable oil, and vanilla extract by whisking them together.
- Mix the dry and liquid parts until the batter is thoroughly mixed.

- Take an 8-inch diameter cake pan. First, spray a cake pan with cooking spray to grease it, and then pour the batter into the pan.
- After that, place it inside the air fryer to cook.
- Start the air fryer cooking by pre-setting it for 18–20 minutes.
- Put a toothpick in the center to check if the cake is made.
- Take the baking pan from the air fryer and let it cool for a few minutes.
- Sprinkle some powdered sugar on the cake's top, then serve.

Variations:

- Add chocolate chunks or chopped nuts if you want the batter to have more texture.
- If you want your cake to have a mocha flavor, add one tablespoon of instant coffee or espresso powder to the mixture before baking.

Air Fryer Blueberry Muffins

- Preparation Time: 10 minutes
- Cooking Time: 12-15 minutes
- Serving Size: 4

Nutrition Facts (per serving):

- Calories: 420
- Fat: 20g
- Protein: 5g
- Fiber: 2g

Ingredients:

- All-purpose flour - 2 cups
- Baking powder - 2 tsp
- Salt - 1/4 tsp

- Granulated sugar - 1/2 cup
- Large egg - 1
- Milk - 1 cup
- Vegetable oil - 1/4 cup
- Vanilla extract - 1 tsp
- Blueberries (fresh or frozen) - 1 cup
- Cooking spray

Instructions:

- Put the air fryer into preheating mode and set the temperature to 340°F (170°C) for 5 minutes.
- Mix the all-purpose flour, baking powder, salt, and granulated sugar in a large mixing bowl with a whisk.
- Mix the milk, vanilla extract, egg, and vegetable oil in a separate mixing bowl and whisk until smooth.
- Mix the dry and liquid ingredients until the batter is smooth.
- Now add blueberries and thoroughly combine them with the other ingredients.
- Spray some cooking spray on the muffin cup.
- Fill muffin cups two-thirds with muffin mixture.

- Air fry muffins for 12–15 minutes or until a toothpick inserted into the center comes out clean.
- After a few minutes, remove the muffin cup and let it cool.
- Carefully take the muffins out of the cup and serve hot.

Variations:

- To make lemon blueberry muffins, stir one teaspoon of lemon zest into the mixture.
- If you want a different flavor, try using strawberries or blackberries instead of blueberries in the recipe.
- To accompany the blueberry pancakes, serve whipped cream cheese or honey drizzled over the top.

Air Fryer Banana Bread

- Preparation Time: 10 minutes
- Cooking Time: 30-35 minutes
- Serving Size: 4

Ingredients:

- All-purpose flour - 1 1/2 cups
- Baking powder - 1 tsp
- Baking soda - 1/2 tsp
- Salt - 1/4 tsp
- Ground cinnamon - 1/2 tsp
- Ripe bananas - 3
- Granulated sugar - 1/2 cup
- Large egg - 1

- Vegetable oil - 1/4 cup
- Vanilla extract - 1 tsp
- Chopped walnuts (optional) - 1/2 cup
- Cooking spray

Instructions:

- Put the air fryer into preheating mode and set the temperature to 320°F (160°C) for 5 minutes.
- With the help of a whisk, Mix all-purpose flour, baking soda, baking powder, ground cinnamon, and salt in a mixing bowl.
- Smash the ripe bananas with a fork and place them in a separate mixing bowl.
- Mix the mashed bananas with the granulated sugar, egg, oil, and vanilla essence.
- Mix the dry and liquid parts until the batter is thoroughly mixed.
- If you want to add crushed walnuts, Add it here
- Take a 7-inch cake pan. Grease a cake pan with cooking spray and then pour the batter inside.
- Now place it inside the air fryer.
- Set the air fryer to 30-35 minutes and start cooking

- To determine whether or not the cake is made, stick a toothpick into the center of the cake.
- Carefully remove banana bread from the cake pan before cutting it into pieces. Serve.

Variations:

- To make chocolate banana bread, stir in one tablespoon of cocoa powder before baking.
- Try substituting chocolate chunks for the walnuts in this recipe for a sweeter finish.
- To make banana bread with a spicy kick, stir one teaspoon of powdered ginger into the batter.
- If you'd like, you can serve the banana bread with a dollop of caramel sauce or vanilla ice cream.

Air Fryer Lemon Bars

- Preparation Time: 15 minutes
- Cooking Time: 18-20 minutes
- Serving Size: 4

Nutrition Facts (per serving):

- Calories: 380
- Fat: 20g
- Protein: 4g
- Fiber: 1g

Ingredients:

- All-purpose flour - 1 cup
- Powdered sugar - 1/4 cup
- Salt - 1/4 tsp

- Unsalted butter - 1/2 cup, cold and cut into small cubes
- Large egg yolks - 2
- Granulated sugar - 1 cup
- Lemon zest - 2 tsp
- Lemon juice - 1/2 cup
- All-purpose flour - 2 tbsp
- Powdered sugar - for dusting

Instructions:

- Put the air fryer into preheating mode and set the temperature to 325°F (165°C) for 5 minutes.
- Mix unsalted butter, powdered sugar, and salt in a bowl. Continue to combine everything by thoroughly mixing it.
- Mix flour into the butter mixture until a dough forms.
- Now properly divide the crumb mixture as you press it into the bottom of an 8x8 inch baking dish.
- Place the cake pan in the air fryer.
- Set the air fryer to 10 minutes and start cooking.
- In a separate mixing dish, combine the large egg yolks, granulated sugar, lemon zest, lemon juice, and

all-purpose flour by whisking the ingredients together until they are thoroughly combined.
- Now, pour the lemon mixture on top of the partially baked crust.
- Return the baking dish to the air fryer and continue cooking for 8 to 10 minutes or until the lemon concoction has reached the desired consistency.
- Take the baking dish from the air fryer and set it aside for a few minutes to settle down.
- After cutting them into squares, sprinkle powdered sugar on top of the lemon cookies.
- They are now prepared and ready to serve.

Variations:

- To give them a different texture, you can top the lemon squares with whipped cream or meringue.
- Before air-frying, for a more tropical take on the dish, sprinkle some shredded coconut on top of the lemon combination.

Air Fryer Carrot Cake

- Preparation Time: 15 minutes
- Cooking Time: 25-30 minutes
- Serving Size: 4

Nutrition Facts (per serving):

- Calories: 470
- Fat: 30g
- Protein: 5g
- Fiber: 3g

Ingredients:

- All-purpose flour - 1 cup
- Baking powder - 1 tsp
- Baking soda - 1/2 tsp

- Ground cinnamon - 1 tsp
- Salt - 1/4 tsp
- Large eggs - 2
- Granulated sugar - 3/4 cup
- Vegetable oil - 1/2 cup
- Vanilla extract - 1 tsp
- Grated carrots - 1 1/2 cups
- Chopped walnuts (optional) - 1/2 cup
- Cooking spray

For Cream Cheese Frosting:

- Cream cheese - 4 oz, softened
- Unsalted butter - 2 tbsp, softened
- Powdered sugar - 1 cup
- Vanilla extract - 1 tsp

Instructions:

- Put the air fryer into preheating mode and set the temperature to 350°F (175°C) for 5 minutes.
- Mix all-purpose flour, baking powder, baking soda, ground cinnamon, and salt using a whisk in a mixing bowl.

- In a separate Bowl, mix the large eggs, granulated sugar, vegetable oil, and vanilla extract by whisking the ingredients together until thoroughly mixed.
- Now incorporate the dry ingredients into the liquid ones slowly and gently while stirring constantly until the batter is completely smooth.
- Now, add sliced carrots and chopped walnuts (if using) and gently mix all the ingredients using a spatula or spoon.
- Transfer the batter to the prepared pan after lightly spraying a cake pan measuring 7 inches with cooking spray.
- Add the cake pan to the air fryer. Adjust the timer on the air fryer to between 25 and 30 minutes, and then begin cooking.
- Inserting a toothpick into the center of the cake will tell you if the cake is ready or not.
- Remove the cake carefully and let it cool for a few minutes.

- In a mixing bowl, Mix the softened cream cheese, unsalted butter, powdered sugar, and vanilla essence using a whisk until the mixture is smooth and creamy.
- After the carrot cake has cooled completely, spread the cream cheese frosting all over the top of it.
- Pieced before serving

Variations:

- If you want the texture sweeter, try substituting raisins for the hazelnuts.
- To give the cream cheese frosting a tangy citrus flavor, stir one teaspoon of orange peel into the bowl.
- On top of the cream cheese frosting, sprinkle some shredded coconut for an additional layer of flavor and a different kind of substance.

Air Fryer S'mores

- Preparation Time: 5 minutes
- Cooking Time: 3-5 minutes
- Serving Size: 4

Nutrition Facts (per serving):

- Calories: 150
- Fat: 6g
- Protein: 1g
- Fiber: 1g

Ingredients:

- Graham crackers - 8 whole crackers broken into halves

- Milk chocolate bars - 4 bars, broken into squares
- Large marshmallows - 8 marshmallows

Instructions:

- On a microwave-safe plate, microwave the marshmallows for 10-15 seconds until they become soft and gooey.
- Place four Graham cracker halves on a baking sheet and top each with a chocolate square.
- On top of the square of chocolate, place a marshmallow.
- Top each marshmallow with another Graham cracker half to create a sandwich.
- Put the baking sheet in the air fryer and air fry for 3 to 5 minutes or until the marshmallows have reached the desired level of toastiness.
- Take the baking sheet out of the air fryer and give the s'mores a few moments to settle down after taking it out.
- Serve Hot.

Variations:

- Try substituting milk chocolate squares with dark or white chocolate squares for a more varied range of flavor profiles.
- Try topping them with a sliver of banana or a few strawberry pieces for natural sweetness in your s'mores.
- For a one-of-a-kind spin on this recipe, try using sweetened marshmallows like caramel or vanilla.
- For a variation on the traditional base, try using chocolate chip cookies or shortbread biscuits instead of graham crackers.

Air Fryer Peanut Butter Cookies

- Preparation Time: 15 minutes
- Cooking Time: 8-10 minutes
- Serving Size: 4

Ingredients:

- All-purpose flour - 1 cup
- Baking soda - 1/2 tsp
- Salt - 1/4 tsp
- Unsalted butter - 1/2 cup, softened
- Granulated sugar - 1/2 cup
- Brown sugar - 1/2 cup, packed
- Creamy peanut butter - 1/2 cup

- Large egg - 1
- Vanilla extract - 1 tsp

Instructions:

- Put the air fryer into preheating mode and set the temperature to 350°F (175°C) for 5 minutes.
- Mix all-purpose flour, baking soda, and salt in a mixing bowl using a whisk.
- In a separate mixing bowl, use a hand mixer to beat the softened unsalted butter, granulated sugar, brown sugar, and creamy peanut butter until they are fluffy and light.
- Now add a large egg and vanilla essence to the mixture made with the butter and beat it until everything is thoroughly combined.
- Gradually mix the dry and wet ingredients and stir until the cookie dough is smooth.
- Roll the cookie dough into balls approximately one inch in diameter and place them on a baking sheet lined with parchment paper.

- Make a crisscross pattern on each ball by pressing down on it with a fork.
- Put the baking sheet into the air fryer for 8 to 10 minutes or until the sides of the cookies are light golden brown.
- Take the baking sheet out of the air fryer, and then wait a few minutes for the cookies to settle down before serving them.

Variations:

- For a crispier finish, add chopped peanuts to the cookie batter.
- Drizzle melted chocolate over the biscuits after cooling completely for an extra sweet touch.
- If you want to experiment with a new flavor character, try substituting almond or cashew butter for peanut butter.
- Roll the cookie dough pieces in granulated or cinnamon sugar for an extra dose of sweetness and a different kind of crunch.

Air Fryer Chocolate-covered Strawberries

- Preparation Time: 10 minutes
- Cooking Time: 5 minutes
- Serving Size: 4

Nutrition Facts (per serving):

- Calories: 160
- Fat: 10g
- Protein: 1g
- Fiber: 2g

Ingredients:

- Fresh strawberries - 12 strawberries
- Semi-sweet chocolate chips - 1 cup
- Coconut oil - 1 tbsp

Instructions:

- Put the air fryer into preheating mode and set the temperature to 350°F (175°C) for 5 minutes.
- After giving the fresh strawberries a quick rinse, wipe them thoroughly with a paper towel.
- Microwave the semi-sweet chocolate chips and coconut oil in a bowl suitable for the microwave for one to two minutes, stirring every 30 seconds, until the chocolate is completely melted and smooth.
- Now dip each strawberry in the melted chocolate mixture, and place the strawberries on a baking sheet coated with parchment paper.
- Transfer the baking sheet to the air fryer after coating all the strawberries with chocolate.
- Fry the chocolate-coated strawberries in an air fryer for 5 minutes or until they are glossy and solid.

- Remove the baking sheet from the air fryer and let the chocolate-wrapped strawberries cool for a few minutes before serving.

Variations:

- If you want something new flavor-wise, try substituting white or dark chocolate chunks for semi-sweet chocolate chips.
- You can also serve the chocolate-coated strawberries with whipped cream or ice cream.

Air Fryer Cinnamon Rolls

- Preparation Time: 20 minutes
- Cooking Time: 10-12 minutes
- Serving Size: 4

Nutrition Facts (per serving):

- Calories: 320
- Fat: 18g
- Protein: 3g
- Fiber: 1g

Ingredients:

- 1 can refrigerated cinnamon roll dough
- Cooking spray

Instructions:

- Put the air fryer into preheating mode and set the temperature to 350°F (175°C) for 5 minutes.
- Unroll refrigerated cinnamon roll dough on a flat surface.
- Create four equal portions of the dough by slicing it with a sharp knife or snipping it with scissors.
- Spray some cooking spray onto the receptacle of the air fryer.
- Place the cinnamon roll pieces into the basket of the air fryer, allowing some room between each piece.
- Fry the cinnamon rolls in an air fryer for 10 to 12 minutes or until they have a golden brown color all the way through and are thoroughly cooked in the middle.
- After the cinnamon rolls have finished cooking in the air fryer, remove them and set them aside to cool.
- Serve the cinnamon roll with a little coating of icing on top.

Variations:

- Before air-frying, the cinnamon rolls enhance their structure and flavor by topping them with chopped nuts, raisins, or other dried fruit.
- To achieve a smoother consistency, combine cream cheese with the frosting in the package.
- If you want the cinnamon sugar combination to have a more nuanced flavor, try adding some nutmeg or ginger.
- The cinnamon rolls can be served as an indulgent dessert option with a dollop of vanilla ice cream on top.

Air Fryer Red Velvet Cake

- Preparation Time: 15 minutes
- Cooking Time: 30-35 minutes
- Serving Size: 4

Nutrition Facts (per serving):

- Calories: 520
- Fat: 28g
- Protein: 6g
- Fiber: 2g

Ingredients:

- All-purpose flour - 1 cup
- Granulated sugar - 1 cup
- Baking powder - 1 tsp
- Baking soda - 1 tsp
- Salt - 1/4 tsp
- Unsweetened cocoa powder - 2 tbsp
- Buttermilk - 1/2 cup
- Vegetable oil - 1/2 cup
- Large eggs - 2
- Red food coloring - 2 tbsp
- Vanilla extract - 1 tsp
- Cream cheese frosting - 1 cup

Instructions:

- Put the air fryer into preheating mode and set the temperature to 350°F (175°C) for 5 minutes.
- In a large bowl, all-purpose flour, sugar, baking powder, soda, salt, and unsweetened cocoa powder are whisked together to form the batter for the brownies.
- In a separate mixing dish, whisk the buttermilk, vegetable oil, eggs, red food coloring, and vanilla extract together.
- Blend the dry and wet ingredients together in stages, stirring constantly, until everything is well combined and silky smooth.
- Grease an 8-inch-diameter cake pan, then spoon the cake batter into the prepared pan.
- Place the cake pan in the preheated air fryer.
- Start the cooking process by adjusting the timer on the air fryer to 30–35 minutes.
- Inserting a toothpick into the center of the cake will tell you if the cake is ready or not.

- Take the cake pan out of the air fryer and put it to the side to cool down.
- Ice the cake with cream cheese frosting after it cools.
- Cut into pieces, and serve.

Variations:

- For flavor, add some chopped pecans or walnuts.
- If you want a less complicated confection, you can skip the frosting and sprinkle powdered sugar over the top of the cake.
- Use a different variety of frosting, such as chocolate or vanilla, for a new spin on the traditional recipe.
- For an extra burst of freshness, serve the cake with freshly whipped cream or a topping of fresh cherries.

Air Fryer Peach Cobbler

- Preparation Time: 15 minutes
- Cooking Time: 25-30 minutes
- Serving Size: 4

Nutrition Facts (per serving):

- Calories: 420
- Fat: 20g
- Protein: 4g
- Fiber: 3g

Ingredients:

- Fresh peaches - 4 cups (peeled, pitted, and sliced)
- All-purpose flour - 1 cup

- Granulated sugar - 1 cup
- Baking powder - 1 tsp
- Salt - 1/4 tsp
- Cinnamon - 1 tsp
- Nutmeg - 1/4 tsp
- Milk - 1 cup
- Unsalted butter - 1/2 cup (melted)
- Vanilla extract - 1 tsp
- Whipped cream or vanilla ice cream - for serving

Instructions:

- Put the air fryer into preheating mode and set the temperature to 350°F (175°C) for 5 minutes.
- Mix all-purpose flour, baking powder, granulated sugar, nutmeg, cinnamon, and salt in a bowl. Mix ingredients thoroughly.
- Mix the milk, melted unsalted butter, and vanilla extract together in a bowl for mixing, and then stir the mixture until it is completely smooth and well combined.
- First, grease an 8-inch-diameter baking dish with butter, and then transfer the batter to the dish using a spoon.

- Spread the peach slices in a decorative pattern on top of the batter.
- Now position your baking dish into the air fryer basket.
- Cook the peach cobbler in an air fryer for 25 to 30 minutes or until the top is golden brown and the peaches have reached the desired tenderness.
- Take the baking dish out of the air fryer, and after a few minutes, the cobbler will be ready to be served.
- Finish your dessert with whipped cream or vanilla ice cream.

Variations:

- If fresh peaches are not available, you can substitute canned peaches instead.
- For an extra crunch, chop nuts like pecans or almonds and fold them into the mixture before baking.
- For a more nutritious take on the traditional dessert, sprinkle some oatmeal over the top of the cobbler.

Air Fryer Pound Cake

- Preparation Time: 15 minutes
- Cooking Time: 35-40 minutes
- Serving Size: 4

Nutrition Facts (per serving):

- Calories: 560
- Fat: 30g
- Protein: 10g
- Fiber: 1g

Ingredients:

- All-purpose flour - 2 cups
- Baking powder - 2 tsp
- Salt - 1/4 tsp
- Unsalted butter - 1 cup (at room temperature)
- Granulated sugar - 1 1/2 cups
- Large eggs - 4
- Vanilla extract - 2 tsp
- Milk - 1/2 cup

Instructions:

- Put the air fryer into preheating mode and set the temperature to 350°F (175°C) for 5 minutes.
- Whisk the baking powder, salt, and all-purpose flour in a mixing bowl.
- In a separate bowl, beat the unsalted butter and granulated sugar together until they are fluffy and well blended.
- Slowly Add eggs one at a time to the mixture, mixing well before adding the next. This will keep the mixture smooth and consistent.
- Now add vanilla extract to the mixture.
- Add the flour mixture to the butter mixture in stages, alternating with the milk, and mix until all ingredients have been thoroughly mixed and smooth.
- First, prepare a baking dish with a diameter of 8 inches by greasing it, and then use a spoon to transfer the batter into the greased baking dish.
- Put the cake pan into the air fryer and start the process.

- Start the cooking process by adjusting the air fryer's timer to 30–35 minutes.
- To find out if the cake is done, just stick a toothpick in the middle of it. If the toothpick comes out clean, the cake is ready to be served.
- After cooking, remove the bread from the air fryer and set it aside for a few minutes to cool down before slicing and serving it.

Variations:

- Add freshly squeezed orange or lemon juice to give the batter a citrus flavor.
- Before baking, add one teaspoon of cinnamon or nutmeg for flavor.
- I frosted the pound cake with whipped cream and fresh berries to give it a fruity touch.
- For an additional sweet touch, drizzle melted chocolate or caramel syrup over the pound cake before serving.

Air Fryer Oreo Cheesecake

- Preparation Time: 15 minutes
- Cooking Time: 35-40 minutes
- Chilling Time: 2-3 hours
- Serving Size: 4

Nutrition Facts (per serving):

- Calories: 480
- Fat: 35g
- Protein: 8g
- Fiber: 1g

Ingredients:

- Oreo cookies - 20
- Unsalted butter - 4 tbsp (melted)
- Cream cheese - 16 oz (at room temperature)
- Granulated sugar - 1/2 cup
- Large eggs - 2
- Vanilla extract - 1 tsp
- Sour cream - 1/4 cup

Instructions:

- Put the air fryer into preheating mode and set the temperature to 350°F (175°C) for 5 minutes.
- Crush the Oreo cookies into a powder using a food processor until they reach the consistency of a fine powder.
- Mix the melted unsalted butter into the Oreo crumbs until evenly mixed.
- After greasing a springform pan with a diameter of 7 inches, place the Oreo mixture into the bottom of the pan.
- In a bowl with a mixer, whip the cream cheese until it is silky smooth and creamy.
- Add the granulated sugar and continue to beat the mixture until it is thoroughly combined.
- Add eggs one at a time, and ensure the batter is thoroughly combined after each addition.
- Incorporate the vanilla essence as well as the sour cream.
- The cheesecake filling should be poured over the Oreo crust prepared in the springform container.
- Insert the springform plate into the air fryer basket.

- Cook the cheesecake for 35 to 40 minutes, or until the edges are firm and the center only slightly jiggles. This will produce the perfect air-fried cheesecake.
- Take the springform plate out of the air fryer, and once the cheesecake has reached room temperature, you can serve it.
- Before serving, refrigerate the cheesecake for 2–3 hours.

Variations:

- Mix in finely chopped nuts like walnuts or pecans to give the crust more bite.
- As a finishing flourish, decorate the cheesecake with whipped cream and Oreo cookies that have been crushed.
- Drizzle melted chocolate or caramel syrup over the cheesecake before serving for an additional sweet touch.

Air Fryer Nutella Brownies

- Preparation Time: 10 minutes
- Cooking Time: 20-25 minutes
- Serving Size: 4

Nutrition Facts (per serving):

- Calories: 480
- Fat: 30g
- Protein: 6g
- Fiber: 3g

Ingredients:

- Nutella - 1 cup
- Unsalted butter - 1/2 cup (melted)
- Granulated sugar - 1/2 cup;
- Large eggs - 2
- All-purpose flour - 1/2 cup
- Cocoa powder - 1/4 cup
- Baking powder - 1/2 tsp
- Salt - 1/4 tsp
- Chopped hazelnuts (optional) - 1/4 cup

Instructions:

- Put the air fryer into preheating mode and set the temperature to 350°F (175°C) for 5 minutes.
- Mix the nutella, melted unsalted butter, egg, and granulated sugar in a bowl. To properly mix all ingredients,
- Mix the salt, baking powder, and cocoa powder. After that, add all-purpose flour. Whisk the items together until they are all mixed together to ensure there are no clumps.
- Mix the dry ingredients with the Nutella mixture until they are almost entirely mixed.
- If you want crushed hazelnuts, add them in at this point.

- To get started, generously grease a 6-inch square baking pan with your preferred cooking spray.
- Spread brownie batter in pan.
- Next, carefully place the baking pan into the air fryer basket.
- Set the temperature of your air fryer to 350 degrees Fahrenheit, and cook the brownies for 20 to 25 minutes. Place a toothpick in the center and remove when clean to check for doneness.
- After cooking, let the brownies cool for a few minutes before serving.
- Enjoy your perfectly cooked and deliciously gooey brownies!

Variations:

- Add chocolate chunks or chopped chocolate for more flavor.
- Warm chocolate sauce or Nutella can be poured over brownies.

- Whipped cream or vanilla ice cream can be added to the brownies.
- If you want to make the brownies gluten-free, you can replace the all-purpose flour with almond or coconut flour.

Air Fryer Apple Pie

- Preparation Time: 15 minutes
- Cooking Time: 25-30 minutes
- Serving Size: 4

Nutrition Facts (per serving):

- Calories: 380
- Fat: 18g
- Protein: 3g
- Fiber: 4g

Ingredients:

- Pie crust - 1 (store-bought or homemade)
- Apples (peeled, cored, and sliced) - 4 cups
- Granulated sugar - 1/2 cup
- Ground cinnamon - 1 tsp
- Ground nutmeg - 1/4 tsp
- Cornstarch - 2 tbsp
- Lemon juice - 1 tbsp
- Unsalted butter - 2 tbsp. (cut into small pieces)
- Egg - 1 (beaten)
- Coarse sugar - 1 tbsp (optional)

Instructions:

- Put the air fryer into preheating mode and set the temperature to 375°F (190°C) for 5 minutes.
- To prepare the pie crust for your air fryer, dust a flat surface with flour and gently roll out the dough. Then, use a circular cookie cutter or a knife to create circles that will fit perfectly in your air fryer basket.
- Spray some cooking spray onto the receptacle of the air fryer and place the pie crust circles into the basket.
- Mix the sliced apples, granulated sugar, ground cinnamon, powdered nutmeg, cornflour, and lemon juice until evenly combined.

- Place a spoonful of the apple mixture onto each circular pie crust, leaving a border of one inch all the way around.
- Place a few pats of unsalted butter in various locations on the fruits.
- Fold the pie dough's edges over the apples to achieve a more rustic appearance for the pie crust.
- Brush the beaten egg around the outside of the pie crust and then sprinkle with coarse sugar. (Optional)
- Cook the apple pies in the oven at 350°F for 25 to 30 minutes, or until the crust is golden brown and the apples are soft.

Variations:

- Add chopped walnuts or pecans for crunch.
- Serve apple pies with vanilla ice cream or whipped cream.
- For a fancier pie, use a lattice or braided crust.
- Substitute pears for the apples to make a pear pie instead.

Air Fryer Bread Pudding

- Preparation Time: 15 minutes
- Cooking Time: 25-30 minutes
- Serving Size: 4

Nutrition Facts (per serving):

- Calories: 550
- Fat: 30g
- Protein: 11g
- Fiber: 2g

Ingredients:

- Sliced bread (cut into cubes) - 6 cups
- Milk - 2 cups
- Heavy cream - 1 cup
- Granulated sugar - 1 cup
- Eggs - 3
- Vanilla extract - 2 tsp
- Ground cinnamon - 1 tsp
- Salt - 1/4 tsp
- Unsalted butter - 2 tbsp (melted)
- Raisins (optional) - 1/2 cup

Instructions:

- Put the air fryer into preheating mode and set the temperature to 375°F (190°C) for 5 minutes.
- In a large bowl, combine the milk, heavy cream, granulated sugar, eggs, vanilla essence, ground cinnamon, and salt by whisking the ingredients together.
- Add bread cubes and raisins(if using) to the bowl, and mix everything together until the mixture evenly covers the bread.
- Spray some cooking spray into a baking container that can fit into the basket of your air fryer.

- Pouring the bread mixture into the baking dish, add unsalted, melted butter.
- Put the baking dish into the air fryer, and cook it for 25 to 30 minutes, or until the pudding has reached the desired consistency and the top is golden brown.
- After removing the baking dish from the air fryer, wait a few minutes for it to settle down before serving the food.

Variations

- Add chopped pecans or almonds to the bread mixture for texture.
- Before serving, pour caramel sauce or sprinkle bread pudding with powdered sugar.

Air Fryer Pumpkin Pie

- Preparation Time: 20 minutes
- Cooking Time: 45-50 minutes
- Serving Size: 8

Nutrition Facts (per serving):

- Calories: 280
- Fat: 10g
- Protein: 6g
- Fiber: 2g

Ingredients:

- Pie crust (9-inch) - 1
- Pumpkin puree - 1 can (15 oz)
- Evaporated milk - 1 can (12 oz)
- Large eggs - 2

- Brown sugar - 3/4 cup
- Ground cinnamon - 1 tsp
- Ground ginger - 1 tsp
- Ground nutmeg - 1/2 tsp
- Salt - 1/4 tsp
- Whipped cream (optional)

Instructions:

- Put the air fryer into preheating mode and set the temperature to 350°F (175°C) for 5 minutes.
- For a delicious pumpkin filling, combine the pumpkin puree, evaporated milk, eggs, brown sugar, ground cinnamon, ground ginger, ground nutmeg, and salt in a large mixing bowl. Whisk the ingredients until smooth and well mixed.
- Pour the pumpkin mixture into the pie shell, and use a spatula to even out the surface of the filling.
- After placing the pie in the basket of the air fryer, air-fry it for 45 to 50 minutes, or until the center has set and a toothpick inserted in the middle yields clean results.

- Take the pie out of the air fryer, and before serving it, let it cool to room temperature on its own.
- Before serving, add whipped cream on top (though this step is optional).

Variations:

- Add oats, flour, butter, and brown sugar crumble for texture and flavor.
- Instead of a pie crust, use Graham crackers.
- Heavy cream makes pumpkin pie creamier.
- Spice up the pumpkin mixture with a pinch of cloves.

Air Fryer Chocolate Fudge

- Preparation Time: 10 minutes
- Cooking Time: 1 hour and 30 minutes
- Serving Size: 16

Nutrition Facts (per serving):

- Calories: 230
- Fat: 14g
- Protein: 2g
- Fiber: 2g

Ingredients:

- Sweetened condensed milk - 1 can (14 oz)
- Semi-sweet chocolate chips - 2 cups

- Unsalted butter - 1/4 cup, cut into small pieces
- Vanilla extract - 1 tsp
- Salt - 1/4 tsp
- Chopped nuts or sprinkles for topping (optional)

Instructions:

- To prepare your 8-inch baking dish, line it with Baking paper and set it aside.
- Mix the chocolate chips, sweetened condensed milk, and unsalted butter together in a microwave-safe bowl.
- Stir the mixture every 30 seconds in the microwave until the chocolate and butter are totally melted and smooth.
- Add vanilla and a touch of salt.
- Mix the vanilla essence and salt thoroughly with a stir-stick.
- Place the chocolate mixture in the baking dish and smooth it out with a spatula to create an even layer.
- Put the baking dish into the air fryer basket for 90 minutes and set the temperature to 250°F (120°C).

- Once done, remove the casserole dish from the air fryer and let the fudge cool. After cooling down, take the fudge out of the baking dish and cut it into 16 pieces.
- Before serving, you can top the dish with chopped nuts or sprinkles.

Variations:

- Before pouring the chocolate mixture into the baking dish, stir in a half cup of creamy peanut butter. This will turn the chocolate combination into chocolate peanut butter fudge.
- Before pouring the chocolate concoction into the baking dish to form cookies and cream fudge, stir one-half cup of crushed Oreos or other cookies into the chocolate mixture.
- Add one teaspoon of instant coffee granules if you want the chocolate to have a mocha flavor.

Air Fryer Chocolate Covered Pretzels

- Preparation Time: 10 minutes
- Cooking Time: 10 minutes
- Serving Size: 4

Nutrition Facts (per serving):

- Calories: 220
- Fat: 12g
- Protein: 3g
- Fiber: 2g

Ingredients:

- Pretzels - 2 cups
- Semi-sweet chocolate chips - 1 cup
- White chocolate chips - 1/2 cup (optional)
- Coconut oil - 1 tbsp
- Toppings of your choice (such as chopped nuts, sprinkles, or sea salt flakes)

Instructions:

- Put the air fryer into preheating mode and set the temperature to 300°F (150°C) for 5 minutes.
- Prepare the basket of the air fryer by lining it with baking paper to keep everything neat and organized.

- Grab a microwave-safe bowl and add semi-sweet chocolate chips and coconut oil. Microwave for 30 seconds, then swirl the mixture until it is smooth. If necessary, continue melting in increments of 15 seconds until it is completely melted in the microwave. Repeat until the chocolate is fully melted.
- Now dip each pretzel in the chocolate mixture. Cover it in chocolate and place it in the air fryer's parchment-lined basket.
- Finish covering all pretzels.
- Put it in an air fryer and cook it for five minutes.
- You can prepare the white chocolate chips while the pretzels are air frying. Place them in a microwave-safe bowl and melt them using the same method you used for the semi-sweet chocolate chips.
- When the air cooking of the pretzels is complete, take them out of the air fryer and allow them to cool.
- Pour melted white chocolate over pretzels and sprinkle garnishes of your choice.
- Wait until the chocolate has thoroughly hardened and cooled before serving.

Variations:

- To give the chocolate a nutty flavor, stir one tablespoon of peanut or almond butter into the warmed chocolate.
- Crush up your go-to candy bar, then distribute the crumbs all over the pretzels coated in chocolate.
- Instead of using semi-sweet chocolate, go for milk or dark chocolate.
- Alternatively, you can give the pretzels a new appearance by dipping them only halfway into the chocolate mixture.
- Use all the different variations of pretzels, such as twists, sticks, and poles.

Air Fryer Rice Krispie Treats

- Preparation Time: 10 minutes
- Cooking Time: 5 minutes
- Serving Size: 6

Nutrition Facts (per serving):

- Calories: 160
- Fat: 4g
- Protein: 1g
- Fiber: 0g

Ingredients:

- Rice Krispies cereal - 4 cups
- Marshmallows - 10 oz
- Unsalted butter - 3 tbsp
- Vanilla extract - 1 tsp
- Cooking spray

Instructions:

- Grab a microwave-safe bowl and add Butter and marshmallows. First heat the mixture for thirty seconds in the microwave, then stir it until it is completely smooth. If it is not completely melted after the first round, repeat the melting process with smaller increments until it is. Continue doing so until the chocolate has completely melted.
- Add the vanilla essence and mix well.
- To create the perfect blend, gently pour the Rice Krispies cereal into the bowl and mix it into the marshmallow mixture until every single piece is coated to perfection.
- Spray some cooking spray onto the receptacle of the air fryer.

- Put the Rice Krispie mixture in the basket of the air fryer, and then press down on it to make sure it is distributed evenly.
- Fry in an air fryer at 350°F (175°C) for 5 minutes or until the top is a light golden brown.
- After removing the air fryer basket, let the Rice Krispie treats cool before cutting and serving them.

Variations:

- For taste and texture, add chocolate chips or chopped nuts.
- Drizzle melted chocolate over cooled Rice Krispie cookies for a delicious touch.
- Use cookie cutters to cut the goodies into designs like hearts or stars after air frying.
- Substitute Fruity Pebbles or Cocoa Krispies for Rice Krispies.
- Add food coloring to the melted marshmallows for a festive touch.

Air Fryer Chocolate Croissants

- Preparation Time: 10 minutes
- Cooking Time: 8 minutes
- Serving Size: 4

Nutrition Facts (per serving):

- Calories: 380
- Fat: 20g
- Protein: 8g
- Fiber: 2g

Ingredients:

- Croissants: 4
- Chocolate Chips: 4 oz.
- Egg: 1 (beaten)

Instructions:

- Put the air fryer into preheating mode and set the temperature to 350°F (175°C) for 5 minutes.
- To prepare your croissants, first cut them in half lengthwise through the middle, and then generously sprinkle one ounce of chocolate chips onto the bottom half of each croissant. This will complete the preparation process.
- Place a small amount of the beaten egg in the center of each of the croissant's four corners.
- Simply layer the top half of the croissant onto the bottom half with the chocolate chips.
- Next, place the croissants in the air fryer basket, leaving enough space between them for even cooking.
- Cook the croissants in an air fryer for 8 minutes or until they have a beautiful brown color.
- Enjoy while it is still warm.

Variations

- Alternately, before air-frying the croissants, you can sprinkle some cinnamon sugar on top of them for an additional layer of flavor.
- Before adding the chocolate chunks, add a dollop of cream cheese or Nutella to the croissants for an additional layer of richness.
- Before serving, dust the dish with powdered sugar to create an attractive presentation.

Air Fryer Baked Apples

- Preparation Time: 10 minutes
- Cooking Time: 20 minutes
- Serving Size: 4

Nutrition Facts (per serving):

- Calories: 140
- Fat: 7g
- Protein: 0g
- Fiber: 2g

Ingredients:

- Medium-sized apples: 4, cored and sliced into 1/2-inch pieces
- Unsalted butter: 2 tbsp, melted
- Brown sugar: 1/4 cup

- Ground cinnamon: 1 teaspoon
- Ground nutmeg: 1/4 tsp.
- Salt: 1/4 tsp

Instructions:

- Put the air fryer into preheating mode and set the temperature to 375°F (190°C) for 5 minutes.
- In a bowl, combine unsalted melted butter and brown sugar, cinnamon, ground nutmeg, and a pinch of salt.
- Place the apple slices in the bowl, and then use your hands to gently toss the apples until each piece is coated in the aromatic mixture. Continue doing this until all of the apple slices are coated.
- Arrange the apple slices in the air fryer basket, leaving some space in between to ensure even cooking.
- Air Fry the apple slices in the air for 10 minutes, turn them over, and cook them for another 10 minutes until they are tender and golden brown.
- Enjoy while it's still fresh.

Variations:

- Add chopped pecans or walnuts to the apple mixture for a bit of crunch.
- Before serving, add a touch of decadence by drizzling caramel sauce over roasted apples and then serving.
- To make a mouthwatering dessert from the roasted apples, top each Serving with a dollop of vanilla ice cream.

Air Fryer Lemon Pound Cake

- Preparation Time: 15 minutes
- Cooking Time: 35 minutes
- Serving Size: 8

Nutrition Facts (per serving):

- Calories: 280
- Fat: 14g
- Protein: 4g
- Fiber: 1g

Ingredients:

- All-purpose flour: 1 1/2 cups
- Baking powder: 1/2 tsp
- Salt: 1/4 tsp
- Unsalted butter: 1/2 cup, softened
- Granulated sugar: 1 cup
- Large eggs: 2
- Vanilla extract: 1 tsp
- Milk: 1/2 cup
- Zest of 2 lemons
- Fresh lemon juice: 2 tbsp
- Powdered sugar for dusting

Instructions:

- Put the air fryer into preheating mode and set the temperature to 320°F (160°C) for 5 minutes.
- Whisk all three ingredients together in a bowl of medium size: flour, baking powder, and salt.
- In a separate bowl, use a hand mixer to beat the butter and sugar together until they are pale and fluffy. Make this with a hand mixer.
- Add one egg to the mixture and beat it until all is combined. Add the other eggs and continue the process. After that, pour in the vanilla essence and give everything a thorough stir.
- Now mix the lemon juice and lemon peel.
- Add batter to a 7-inch cake pan and spread it out evenly.
- Place the cake pan inside the air fryer, set it for 30-35 minutes and start cooking.
- A toothpick inserted into the middle of the cake should come out clean to indicate readiness.
- Let the cake cool for 10 minutes before removing it from the pan.

- After 10 minutes, take the cake out of the pan.
- Sprinkle with confectioners' sugar and cut into 8 squares.
- Enjoy it

Variations:

- Add poppy seeds to the batter for a lemon poppy seed pound cake.
- Lemon blueberry pound cake: add blueberries to the batter.

Air Fryer Chocolate Donuts

- Preparation Time: 15 minutes
- Cooking Time: 10 minutes
- Serving Size: 6

Nutrition Facts (per serving):

- Calories: 190
- Fat: 6g
- Protein: 3g
- Fiber: 1g

Ingredients:

- All-purpose flour: 1 cup
- Unsweetened cocoa powder: 1/4 cup

- Baking powder: 1/2 tsp
- Baking soda: 1/2 tsp
- Salt: 1/4 tsp
- Granulated sugar: 1/2 cup
- Milk: 1/2 cup
- Large egg: 1
- Unsalted butter: 2 tbsp, melted
- Vanilla extract: 1 tsp
- Non-stick cooking spray

For the glaze:

- Powdered sugar: 1/2 cup
- Milk: 1-2 tbsp
- Vanilla extract: 1/4 tsp

Instructions:

- Whisk flour, cocoa powder, baking powder, baking soda, and salt in a medium bowl.
- Add the sugar, milk, egg, melted butter, and vanilla extract to another larger bowl and mix them all together until thoroughly combined.
- Add the flour mixture little by little while mixing it in until it is completely incorporated.

- Put the air fryer into preheating mode and set the temperature to 350°F (175°C) for 5 minutes.
- Spray the doughnut molds with non-stick cooking spray to prevent the doughnuts from sticking to the molds.
- Put the batter into a piping bag or a ziplock bag with one corner cut off, and then pump the batter into the molds so that each mold is only half full.
- Put the mold inside the air fryer.
- Set the air fryer to 8-10 minutes and start cooking.
- A toothpick inserted into the middle of the cake should come out clean to indicate readiness.
- Take the molds out of the air fryer and wait a few minutes for the doughnuts to cool down before removing them from the molded cavities.
- Mix the milk, vanilla essence, and powdered sugar in a small dish to make the glaze and stir until smooth.
- Dip the top of each donut into the glaze and let the excess drip off.
- Put the glazed donuts on a wire rack so that they can cool and the glaze can set for a few minutes.

- Now, your delicious, glazed donuts are ready to be served and enjoyed!

Variations:

- Change flavors using almond or mint extracts.
- Add chopped nuts or chocolate chips to the batter for texture and taste.
- Melt 1/2 cup of chocolate chips with 1/4 cup of heavy cream and dunk the doughnuts in a chocolate ganache glaze.
- Add sprinkles on top of the glaze for a fun and colorful touch.

Air Fryer Cinnamon Apple Chips

- Preparation Time: 10 minutes
- Cooking Time: 15 minutes
- Total Time: 25 minutes
- Serving Size: 4

Nutrition Facts (per serving):

- Calories: 50
- Fat: 0g
- Protein: 0g
- Fiber: 2g

Ingredients:

- Medium apples: 2, thinly sliced
- Ground cinnamon: 1 teaspoon
- Granulated sugar: 1 tablespoon

Instructions:

- Put the air fryer into preheating mode and set the temperature to 350°F (175°C) for 5 minutes.
- In a bowl, thoroughly combine the sugar and cinnamon, mixing until sugar is dissolved.

- Use a mandoline or a sharp knife to cut the apples into thin slices. Ensure that the slices are of uniform thickness to ensure even cooking.
- Place the slices in the air fryer basket in a single layer.
- Enhance the flavor of the apple slices by generously sprinkling them with a blend of sugar and cinnamon.
- Cook the apple chips for 10 to 15 minutes, or until they are crisp and golden brown, turning them over once halfway through the cooking time.
- After air-frying, let the apple chips cool for a few minutes.
- Enjoy the delicious taste of apple chips.

Variations:

- Before air-frying, the apple chips, drizzle some honey on top of them for a sweeter version.
- For various flavors and textures, try using different types of apples like Honeycrisp, Granny Smith, or Gala.

Air Fryer Blueberry Cobbler

- Preparation Time: 15 minutes
- Cooking Time: 25 minutes Total
- Time: 40 minutes
- Serving Size: 4

Nutrition Facts (per serving):

- Calories: 380
- Fat: 16g
- Protein: 4g
- Fiber: 3g

Ingredients:

For the Blueberry Filling:
- Fresh blueberries: 2 cups
- Granulated sugar: 1/4 cup
- Corn starch: 1 tablespoon
- Lemon juice: 1 tablespoon

For the Cobbler Topping:
- All-purpose flour: 1 cup
- Granulated sugar: 1/4 cup
- Brown sugar: 1/4 cup
- Baking powder: 1/2 teaspoon
- Baking soda: 1/4 teaspoon

- Salt: 1/4 teaspoon
- Unsalted butter: 1/2 cup, melted
- Milk: 1/2 cup
- Vanilla extract: 1 teaspoon

Instructions:

- Put the air fryer into preheating mode and set the temperature to 375°F (190°C) for 5 minutes.
- Blueberries, sugar, cornflour, and lemon juice are combined in a medium bowl.
- Combine the sugar, brown sugar, flour, baking soda, baking powder, and salt in a separate bowl. Mix until combined.
- Melt the butter and add it to the bowl with the other ingredients.
- Add the milk and the vanilla essence to the bowl. Stir until all ingredients are thoroughly combined (avoid over-mixing).
- Place spoonfuls of the cobbler topping over the blueberries using a spoon or cookie scoop.

- Put the dish in the air fryer and cook it for 25 to 30 minutes, or until the topping for the cobbler is golden brown and the blueberry filling is bubbly.
- Once done, take it from the air fryer and set it aside for a few minutes to cool down before serving.
- Add whipped cream or vanilla ice cream to blueberry cobbler.

Variations:

- For a different flavor, try substituting raspberries, blackberries, or a combination of different kinds of berries for the blueberries.
- To give the topping of the cobbler a more comforting and homey flavor, try adding some cinnamon or nutmeg.
- Add chopped nuts like almonds or pecans to the topping to give the cobbler a crunchier consistency.
- Replace the all-purpose flour with whole wheat flour, and use coconut sugar or honey instead of granulated sugar for a healthier version.

Air Fryer Oatmeal Cookies

- Preparation Time: 15 minutes
- Cooking Time: 10 minutes per batch
- Total Time: 25 minutes
- Serving Size: 4-6

Nutrition Facts (per serving):

- Calories: 340
- Fat: 16g
- Protein: 4g
- Fiber: 2g

Ingredients:

- Unsalted butter: 1/2 cup, softened
- Brown sugar: 1/2 cup
- Granulated sugar: 1/4 cup
- Egg: 1
- Vanilla extract: 1 teaspoon
- All-purpose flour: 1 cup
- Baking soda: 1/2 teaspoon
- Salt: 1/2 teaspoon
- Rolled oats: 1 cup
- Raisins or chocolate chips: 1/2 cup

Instructions:

- Put the air fryer into preheating mode and set the temperature to 350°F (175°C) for 5 minutes.
- Whisk the softened butter, brown sugar, and granulated sugar in a large bowl until fully combined and fluffy.
- Gently combine the egg and vanilla extract, blending until thoroughly combined in another bowl.
- Mix the flour, baking soda, and salt in a different bowl and whisk until well combined.
- Gradually mix the dry and wet ingredients, and stir until the cookie dough is smooth.
- Mix in the rolled oats, raisins, or chocolate chips(if using).
- Use a cookie scoop or spoon to portion the dough into small balls. Place the balls onto a greased air fryer basket, and space them apart evenly. This will ensure that each cookie is evenly cooked and has enough room to expand while baking.
- Bake for about 10 minutes per batch or until the edges are golden.

- After they have finished cooking, take the cookies from the air fryer and set them aside for a few minutes so that they may cool down.

Variations:

- Substitute chopped almonds or dried cranberries for chocolate chips or raisins for a different taste and texture.
- Try spicing the dough with a teaspoon of cinnamon or nutmeg to give it a more comforting, familiar flavor.
- Make healthier cookies using all-purpose and whole wheat flour.
- Add a quarter cup of raisins or chocolate chips and half a cup of granulated sugar for a sweeter variation.

Air Fryer Peach Dumplings:

- Preparation Time: 15 minutes
- Cooking Time: 18-20 minutes
- Total Time: 33-35 minutes
- Serving Size: 4

Nutrition Facts (per serving):

- Calories: 310
- Fat: 18g
- Protein: 3g
- Fiber: 2g

Ingredients:

- Medium-sized peaches: 2, peeled and sliced
- Unsalted butter: 2 tablespoons
- Brown sugar: 1/4 cup
- Ground cinnamon: 1/2 teaspoon
- Ground nutmeg: 1/4 teaspoon
- Vanilla extract: 1/2 teaspoon
- Frozen puff pastry sheet: 1, thawed
- Egg: 1, beaten
- Vanilla ice cream for serving (optional)

Instructions:

- Put the air fryer into preheating mode and set the temperature to 375°F (190°C) for 5 minutes.
- Melt the butter in a small saucepan set over medium heat until it sizzles.
- Add the sliced peaches, brown sugar, cinnamon, nutmeg, and vanilla extract to the saucepan, stirring until the ingredients are evenly combined.
- Cook the peach mixture for about 7 to 9 minutes, or until the sugar has dissolved and the peaches have become mushy.
- To begin, lightly flour a clean work surface and roll the puff pastry into a rectangular shape.
- Next, cut the pastry into four equal squares using a sharp knife.
- Using a measuring spoon, put a dollop of the peach mixture in the middle of each square.
- Pinch the pastry edges together to seal, then fold the pastry corners over the peach mixture and press together.
- The tops of the pastries should be brushed with the beaten egg.

- Put the peach dumplings in the basket of the air fryer and make sure there is some space between them.
- Cook the dumplings for about 18 to 20 minutes or until they have puffed up and turned a golden brown.
- After the peach dumplings have finished cooking in the air fryer, remove them from the appliance and set them aside to cool for a few minutes before serving.
- Serve peach dumplings warm with vanilla ice cream.

Variations:

- Substitute apples or pears for peaches to change the flavor.
- Scatter chopped nuts or crumbled Graham crackers over the peach mixture before folding the dough for texture and taste. This will hide imperfections.
- Caramel or honey drizzles can sweeten peach dumplings.

Air Fryer Sweet Potato Pie:

- Preparation Time: 15 minutes
- Cooking Time: 35-40 minutes
- Total Time: 50-55 minutes
- Serving Size: 8

Nutrition Facts (per serving):

- Calories: 340
- Fat: 18g
- Protein: 5g
- Fiber: 2g

Ingredients:

For the Pie Crust:

- All-purpose flour: 1 1/4 cups
- Salt: 1/2 teaspoon
- Sugar: 1/2 teaspoon
- Unsalted butter: 1/2 cup, cold and cut into small cubes
- Ice water: 3-5 tablespoons

For the Sweet Potato Filling:

- Medium-sized sweet potatoes: 2, peeled and cubed
- Brown sugar: 3/4 cup
- Large eggs: 2
- Heavy cream: 1/2 cup
- Unsalted butter: 1/4 cup, melted
- Vanilla extract: 1 teaspoon
- Ground cinnamon: 1/2 teaspoon
- Ground nutmeg: 1/4 teaspoon
- Salt: 1/4 teaspoon

Instructions:

- Put the air fryer into preheating mode and set the temperature to 350°F (175°C) for 5 minutes.
- Mix the dry ingredients for the flour, salt, sugar, and pie crust in a large mixing bowl.
- Add cubed pieces to the flour mixture. Use a pastry cutter or fork to blend the ingredients until the mixture forms coarse crumbs.
- To achieve the perfect dough consistency, add the cold water slowly, 1 tablespoon at a time. Keep

adding until the dough comes together and forms a perfect ball.
- To prepare the pie dough for air frying, lightly flour a flat surface and roll out the dough into a circle that is just a touch bigger than your air fryer basket.
- Carefully press pie dough into the air fryer basket's bottom and sides.
- Beat the Eggs and brown sugar until thoroughly combined in a separate mixing bowl.
- Add in the cubed sweet potatoes, heavy cream, melted butter, vanilla extract, ground cinnamon, ground nutmeg, and a pinch of salt until well combined.
- Blend the sweet potato mixture until it reaches a smooth and creamy consistency using either a hand mixer or an immersion blender.
- Once you have prepared the pie crust, pour the sweet potato filling into it. Take care to spread the filling evenly to avoid any clumps. Then, carefully place the sweet potato pie into the air fryer basket.

- Bake the sweet potato pie for 35 to 40 minutes, or until the filling has reached the desired consistency and the crust has become golden brown.
- After the sweet potato pie has finished cooking, remove it from the air fryer and set it aside for a few minutes to cool down before serving.

Variations:

- Before baking, sprinkle chopped nuts over the sweet potato mixture for crunch and flavor.
- Coconut cream replaces heavy cream for a dairy-free pie.
- Mix sweet potatoes with pumpkin puree for a distinct flavor and texture.

Air Fryer Caramel Apples

- Preparation Time: 15 minutes
- Cooking Time: 10-12 minutes
- Total Time: 25-27 minutes
- Serving Size: 4

Nutrition Facts (per serving):

- Calories: 190
- Fat: 5g
- Protein: 1g
- Fiber: 3g

Ingredients:

- Medium-sized apples: 4
- Caramel candies: 1/2 cup, unwrapped

- Water: 1 tablespoon
- Chopped peanuts or other nuts (optional): 1/4 cup

Instructions:

- Put the air fryer into preheating mode and set the temperature to 350°F (175°C) for 5 minutes.
- Clean and dry the apples
- Put a popsicle stick or a skewer made of wood into the core of each apple.
- Mix the caramel candies and water in a microwave safe bowl and put in the microwave.
- To melt the caramels, microwave the mixture on high for 1 minute, stirring every 20 seconds, until the caramels are fully melted.
- Coat each apple thoroughly by dipping it into the melted caramel and coating it thoroughly.
- Place the apples coated in caramel in the basket of the air fryer, leaving some space between each apple.
- Cook the apples in the air fryer for 10 to 12 minutes or until the caramel has reached the desired

consistency and the apples have reached the desired tenderness.
- After they have finished cooking, take the caramel apples out of the air fryer and set them aside for a few minutes to cool down.
- If you'd like, you can sprinkle some chopped nuts over the caramel coating before serving.
- Warm the caramel apples before serving.

Variations:

- For a distinct taste, use melted chocolate or a mixture of caramel and chocolate.
- Try crumbled cookies, coconut flakes, or small marshmallows.
- Use Granny Smith, Honeycrisp, or Fuji apples for varied flavors.

Air Fryer Chocolate Mousse:

- Preparation Time: 15 minutes
- Cooking Time: 10-12 minutes
- Chilling Time: 2-3 hours
- Total Time: 2 hours 30 minutes - 3 hours 27 minutes
- Serving Size: 4

Nutrition Facts (per serving):

- Calories: 290
- Fat: 22g
- Protein: 4g
- Fiber: 2g

Ingredients:

- Semisweet chocolate chips: 4 ounces
- Unsalted butter: 2 tablespoons
- Heavy cream: 2 tablespoons
- Large eggs, separated: 2
- Salt: 1/8 teaspoon
- Cream of tartar: 1/4 teaspoon
- Granulated sugar: 2 tablespoons
- Whipped cream and chocolate shavings for garnish (optional)

Instructions:

- Add chocolate chips, butter, and heavy cream to a microwave-safe bowl.
- Microwave for 1-2 minutes on high, then swirl the mixture until it is smooth. If necessary, continue melting in increments until it is completely melted in the microwave. Repeat until the chocolate is fully melted.
- Add the egg yolks to the mixture when the chocolate is melted and stir until everything is incorporated.
- Beat egg whites, salt, and cream of tartar on high speed in a separate bowl until soft peaks form.
- Add tablespoons of granulated sugar. Keeping egg whites beating. Continue until egg whites form stiff peaks.
- Combine the beaten egg whites with the chocolate in a mixing bowl and stir until no white streaks remain.
- In each of the four ramekins or serving plates, spoon chocolate mousse.
- Place ramekins in the air fryer basket with space between them.

- Cook the chocolate mousse in the air fryer for 10 to 12 minutes or until the mousse has set around the edges but is still slightly jiggly in the center.
- After cooking, cool the chocolate mousse in the air fryer to room temperature before serving.
- Wrap the chocolate mousse in plastic wrap, place it in the refrigerator, and chill for at least 2 to 3 hours or until it has reached the desired consistency.
- After refrigerating, add a touch of elegance to your chocolate mousse by topping it off with a dollop of whipped cream and some delicate chocolate shavings. Savor and enjoy!

Variations:

- Add Grand Marnier or Kahlua to the chocolate for taste.
- To taste different, try dark or milk chocolate instead of semi-sweet.
- Garnish chocolate mousse with fresh fruit or almonds.

Air Fryer Raspberry Cheesecake:

- Preparation Time: 20 minutes
- Cooking Time: 20-25 minutes
- Serving Size: 4

Nutrition Facts (per serving):

- Calories: 380
- Fat: 28g
- Protein: 6g
- Fiber: 2g

Ingredients:

For the crust:

- Graham cracker crumbs: 1 cup
- Unsalted butter: 3 tablespoons, melted
- Granulated sugar: 1 tablespoon

For the Filling:

- Cream cheese: 8 ounces, softened

- Granulated sugar: 1/4 cup
- Large egg: 1
- Sour cream: 1/4 cup
- Vanilla extract: 1/2 teaspoon
- Fresh raspberries, mashed: 1/2 cup

Instructions:

- Put the air fryer into preheating mode and set the temperature to 300°F (150°C) for 5 minutes.
- Add graham cracker crumbs, melted butter, and granulated sugar to a mixing bowl. Stir them well until thoroughly combined.
- Next, Pour the mixture into four ramekins or a 7-inch spring form pan.
- In another bowl, beat cream cheese and granulated sugar on medium speed until smooth.
- Now add the egg, sour cream, and vanilla extract, and continue beating the mixture until everything is thoroughly combined.
- Mix the mashed raspberries into the cream cheese.

- Place a layer of the cream cheese mixture on top of the graham cracker crust in the ramekins or the spring form pan.
- Place spring form pans or ramekins in the air fryer basket with space between them.
- Cook the cheesecake in the air fryer for 20 to 25 minutes or until the outside edges are firm and the middle is just slightly jiggly.
- Take the cheesecake out of the air fryer to cool.
- Wrap the cheesecake in plastic wrap, place it in the refrigerator, and let it chill for at least four hours or overnight until it has reached the desired consistency.
- After chilling enough, remove the cheesecake from the ramekins or springform pan and serve.

Variations:

- Replace raspberries with strawberries, blueberries, or blackberries.
- For a zesty filling, add a tablespoon of lemon juice and zest.

Air Fryer Churros

- Preparation Time: 20 minutes
- Cooking Time: 10-12 minutes
- Total Time: 30 minutes
- Serving Size: 4

Nutrition Facts (per serving):

- Calories: 280
- Fat: 18g
- Protein: 3g
- Fiber: 1g

Ingredients:

- For the Churro Dough:
- Water: 1/2 cup
- Unsalted butter: 2 tablespoons
- Granulated sugar: 1 tablespoon
- Salt: 1/4 teaspoon
- All-purpose flour: 1/2 cup
- Large egg: 1
- Vanilla extract: 1/2 teaspoon
- Granulated sugar: 2 tablespoons
- Ground cinnamon: 1/2 teaspoon

For the Dipping Sauce:

- Semisweet chocolate chips: 1/4 cup
- Heavy cream: 2 tablespoons

Instructions:

- Preheat the air fryer to 375°F (190°C) for 5 minutes.
- To prepare the sauce, start by placing a saucepan over medium heat. Add water, unsalted butter, granulated sugar, and salt to the pan and bring it to a boil.
- After turning the heat down to a low setting, add the all-purpose flour while continuously stirring the

mixture with a wooden spoon until the ingredients form a ball and pull away from the sides of the pan.
- Leave the mixture to cool for 5 minutes.
- Beating the egg properly, adding the vanilla extract, and continue to beat until the mixture is smooth.
- Transfer the mixture to a star-tipped piping bag.
- Carefully pipe the dough onto a piece of parchment paper, forming 4-inch long churros with the piping bag.
- Very lightly spray the churros with cooking spray.
- Put the churros in the air fryer.
- Air-fry the churros for 10-12 minutes until golden brown and crispy.
- While it is cooking in an air fryer, mix granulated sugar and ground cinnamon in a small bowl.
- Once the churros are perfectly cooked in the air fryer, roll them in the cinnamon sugar mixture until they are well coated.
- In another bowl, combine semi-sweet chocolate chips and heavy cream, and microwave the mixture

on high for 30 seconds or until the chocolate is melted, stirring every 10 seconds.
- Finally, serve the churros warm and crispy with velvety melted chocolate sauce for dipping.

Variations:

- Spice up the cinnamon sugar with a pinch of cayenne pepper.
- Dip churros in strawberry or caramel sauce.
- Serve churros with toothpicks at parties.

Air Fryer Almond Flour Chocolate Chip Cookies

- Preparation Time: 10 minutes
- Cooking Time: 8-10 minutes
- Total Time: 20 minutes
- Serving Size: 4

Nutrition Facts (per serving):

- Calories: 220
- Fat: 16g
- Protein: 4g
- Fiber: 2g

Ingredients:

- Almond flour: 1/2 cup
- Coconut sugar: 1/4 cup
- Baking soda: 1/4 teaspoon
- Salt: 1/4 teaspoon
- Melted coconut oil: 1/4 cup
- Egg: 1
- Vanilla extract: 1 teaspoon
- Chocolate chips: 1/4 cup

Instructions:

- Put the air fryer into preheating mode and set the temperature to 350°F (175°C) for 5 minutes.
- Mix almond flour, coconut sugar, baking soda, and salt in a bowl and blend the ingredients well.
- Combine the melted coconut oil, egg, and vanilla extract in a separate bowl with a light hand.
- Mix the dry ingredients in with the wet ones on a step-by-step basis while stirring continuously until the cookie dough is completely smooth.
- Mixing chocolate chips with other ingredients.
- Transfer dough to parchment paper using a cookie scoop.

- Spray the cookies with a very thin coating of cooking spray.
- Put the cookies in the basket of the air fryer, making sure there is enough space between each one to prevent sticking.
- In an air fryer, bake the cookies for 8–10 minutes or until golden brown.
- After air-frying the cookies, let them cool for a few minutes before serving.

Variations:

- Replace chocolate chips with white chocolate chips, raisins, or cranberries.
- For more chocolate, drizzle melted chocolate over cooled cookies.

Air Fryer Apple Cinnamon Cake:

- Preparation Time: 15 minutes
- Cooking Time: 25-30 minutes
- Total Time: 40-45 minutes
- Serving Size: 4

Nutrition Facts (per serving):

- Calories: 300
- Fat: 18g
- Protein: 3g
- Fiber: 2g

Ingredients:

- For the Muffin Batter:
- All-purpose flour: 1/2 cup
- Baking powder: 1/2 teaspoon
- Ground cinnamon: 1/2 teaspoon
- Salt: 1/4 teaspoon
- Unsalted butter (room temperature): 1/4 cup
- Granulated sugar: 1/4 cup
- Large egg: 1
- Vanilla extract: 1/2 teaspoon
- Chopped apple: 1/2 cup

For the Topping:

- Unsalted butter (melted): 2 tablespoons
- All-purpose flour: 1/4 cup
- Brown sugar: 1/4 cup
- Ground cinnamon: 1/2 teaspoon

Instructions:

- Put the air fryer into preheating mode and set the temperature to 350°F (175°C) for 5 minutes.
- To make the flour mixture, whisk together the all-purpose flour, baking powder, cinnamon powder, and salt in a bowl. Mix well.
- In another bowl, cream together unsalted butter and granulated sugar until the mixture becomes fluffy.
- Add the egg and vanilla extract to the mixture and stir until thoroughly combined.
- Next, slowly add the dry and wet ingredients while stirring until smooth. Be careful not to overmix the ingredients.
- Add chopped apples to the mixture.
- Pour the batter into a greased cake pan about 6 inches in diameter.

- Combine the melted unsalted butter, all-purpose flour, brown sugar, and powdered cinnamon until thoroughly mixed.
- Sprinkle the mixture over the cake batter.
- Put it in the air fryer and cook it for 25 to 30 minutes, or until you can test the center with a toothpick and it comes out clean.
- Take the cake from the air fryer and let it rest for a few minutes before cutting it. Enjoy your freshly baked cake!

Variations:

- To give the topping more crunch, chop nuts like pecans or walnuts and add them to the mixture.
- For a different fruit flavor, try substituting chopped pears or peaches for the chopped apple.
- Drizzle caramel sauce or cream cheese frosting over the cooled cake for an even sweeter treat.

Air Fryer Pop Tarts

- Preparation Time: 20 minutes
- Cooking Time: 10-12 minutes
- Total Time: 30-32 minutes
- Serving Size: 4

Nutrition Facts (per serving):

- Calories: 350
- Fat: 18g
- Protein: 3g
- Fiber: 1g

Ingredients:

For the dough:

- All-purpose flour: 1 1/2 cups
- Granulated sugar: 2 tablespoons
- Salt: 1/4 teaspoon
- Unsalted butter: 1/2 cup, cold and cubed
- Ice water: 3-4 tablespoons

For the Filling:

- Jam or fruit preserves of your choice: 1/2 cup

For the Glaze:

- Powdered sugar: 1/2 cup
- Milk: 1 tablespoon
- Vanilla extract: 1/4 teaspoon

Instructions:

- Put the air fryer into preheating mode and set the temperature to 350°F (175°C) for 5 minutes.
- Mix the dry ingredients, all-purpose flour, granulated sugar, and salt in a large bowl and whisk together.

- To mix the butter into the dry ingredients, add cubed unsalted butter and use a pastry blender or fork to cut it in until the texture resembles coarse sand.
- To achieve the perfect dough consistency, add the cold water slowly, 1 tablespoon at a time. Keep adding until the dough comes together and forms a perfect ball.
- Now divide it into two equal parts and gently shape each into a disk. Refrigerate each disk for at least an hour under plastic wrap. This lets the dough rest and firm up, creating a delicious, flaky crust.
- To get started, dust a flat surface with a bit of flour and roll one of the dough disks into a rectangular shape. Cut the dough into 8 equally sized rectangles.
- Next, take 4 rectangles and add a tablespoon of your chosen jam or fruit preserve on top, leaving about 1/2 inch of space along the edges.
- To complete the process, place the remaining 4 rectangles of dough over the jam-filled pieces and use a fork to press down and seal the edges of the dough together.

- Prepare your air fryer by lightly spraying it with cooking spray.
- Put pop tarts in the air fryer basket with space between them.
- Air-fry pop tarts for 10-12 minutes until golden brown.
- Let the pop tarts cool for a few minutes before glazing them with your favorite glaze.

For the glaze:

- In a bowl, combine the powdered sugar, milk, and vanilla essence by whisking the ingredients together until smooth.
- Once your pop tarts have cooled down, drizzle the glaze carefully over each one. This glaze's sweet and creamy taste will make your pop-tarts irresistible!

Variations:

- Try using different kinds of jam or fruit preserves when making pop-tarts with various flavors.
- Try sprinkling some cinnamon or nutmeg to give the dough a flavor reminiscent of warm spices.
- For an even more decadent dessert, drizzle melted chocolate or caramel sauce over pop tarts and let them cool.

Air Fryer Chocolate Covered Bananas

- Preparation Time: 10 minutes
- Cooking Time: 5 minutes
- Total Time: 15 minutes
- Serving Size: 4

Nutrition Facts (per serving):

- Calories: 180
- Fat: 12g
- Protein: 2g
- Fiber: 2g

Ingredients:

- Bananas: 2, peeled and cut into 1-inch pieces
- Semisweet chocolate chips: 4 ounces
- Coconut oil: 2 tablespoons
- Your choice of toppings, such as chopped nuts, shredded coconut, or sprinkles

Instructions:

- Put the air fryer into preheating mode and set the temperature to 350°F (175°C) for 5 minutes.

- To prepare the chocolate mixture, grab a microwave-safe bowl and add semisweet chocolate chips and coconut oil.
- To melt and smooth the chocolate, microwave the two ingredients for 30 seconds, stirring between breaks.
- To coat each banana with chocolate, dip it in the melted chocolate and then use a fork to spread the chocolate evenly over the banana.
- Place the slices of chocolate-covered banana on a dish covered with parchment paper.
- Sprinkle the toppings of your choice over the bananas coated in chocolate.
- Put the plate of chocolate-covered bananas into the air fryer, and cook them for about 4 to 5 minutes or until the chocolate has set.
- When the chocolate has hardened to the desired consistency, remove the plate from the air fryer and wait a few minutes for the chocolate-covered bananas to cool before serving.

Variations:

- If you want the chocolate to have a more interesting flavor, try melting it with sea salt or cinnamon.
- Use a variety of toppings, such as crushed graham crackers, miniature chocolate chips, or chopped dried fruit.

Air Fryer Zucchini Bread

- Preparation Time: 20 minutes
- Cooking Time: 50 minutes
- Total Time: 1 hour, 10 minutes
- Serving Size: 8-10 slices

Nutrition Facts (per serving):

- Calories: 250
- Fat: 12g
- Protein: 3g
- Fiber: 2g

Ingredients:

- Grated zucchini: 1 cup
- All-purpose flour: 1 cup
- Whole wheat flour: 1/2 cup
- Granulated sugar: 1/2 cup
- Brown sugar: 1/2 cup
- Vegetable oil: 1/2 cup
- Large eggs: 2
- Vanilla extract: 1 teaspoon
- Baking powder: 1 teaspoon
- Baking soda: 1/2 teaspoon
- Salt: 1/2 teaspoon
- Ground cinnamon: 1/2 teaspoon
- Cooking spray

Instructions:

- Put the air fryer into preheating mode and set the temperature to 320°F (160°C) for 5 minutes.
- In a large bowl, mix whole wheat flour, all-purpose flour, baking soda, baking powder, salt, and cinnamon. To combine the ingredients, give the mixture a thorough whisking.
- The next step is to take a second mixing bowl and use a whisk to combine the granulated sugar, brown sugar, vegetable oil, eggs, and vanilla extract until the mixture is uniform and smooth.

- To the wet ingredients, add the grated zucchini, and combine everything thoroughly.
- Gradually mix the dry and wet ingredients, and stir until the cookie dough is smooth.
- Begin by spraying a 6-inch loaf pan with cooking spray, ensuring the entire surface is lightly coated to prevent the batter from sticking.
- Distribute the zucchini bread batter evenly in the prepared pan.
- Place the cake pan in the air fryer.
- Set the air fryer to 30-35 minutes and start cooking
- The cake is done when a toothpick inserted into its center comes out clean.
- Once done, remove from the air fryer and let it cool for a few minutes.
- After cooling, remove it from pan and slice the bread into desired portions.

Variations:

- A half cup of chopped walnuts or pecans adds crunch to the batter.
- Change the taste by using nutmeg or pumpkin pie spice for cinnamon.

Air Fryer Lemon Poppyseed Muffins

- Preparation Time: 15 minutes
- Cooking Time: 12 minutes
- Total Time: 27 minutes
- Serving Size: 6 muffins

Nutrition Facts (per serving):

- Calories: 180
- Fat: 9g
- Protein: 3g
- Fiber: 1g

Ingredients:

- All-purpose flour: 1 cup
- Granulated sugar: 1/4 cup
- Poppyseeds: 2 tablespoons
- Baking powder: 1 teaspoon
- Baking soda: 1/4 teaspoon
- Salt: 1/4 teaspoon
- Milk: 1/2 cup
- Vegetable oil: 1/4 cup
- Egg: 1
- Lemon zest: 1 tablespoon
- Lemon juice: 1 tablespoon
- Cooking spray

Instructions:

- Put the air fryer into preheating mode and set the temperature to 350°F (175°C) for 5 minutes.
- To make the batter, combine the all-purpose flour, granulated sugar, poppy seeds, baking powder, baking soda, and salt in a mixing bowl. Stir the ingredients in a bowl until well combined.
- Mix the milk, vegetable oil, egg, lemon zest, and lemon juice in a separate dish using a whisk. Keep whisking until all the ingredients are fully incorporated.

- Gradually mix the dry and wet ingredients and stir until the cookie dough is smooth.
- Spray a muffin tray with cooking spray, then divide the batter between the 6 cups of the tin to be uniformly distributed.
- Place the cake pan in the air fryer.
- Set the air fryer to 10-12 minutes and start cooking.
- Insert a toothpick into the cake; it is fully cooked if it doesn't stick.
- Remove it from the air fryer and wait for it to cool down before removing it from the pan.

Variations:

- Add 1/4 cup of chopped nuts, like almonds or pecans, to give the batter more crunch.
- If you want a different flavor, try substituting lime or orange zest and juice for the lemon zest and juice.
- Applying a glaze made of powdered sugar and lemon juice to the top of the muffins will make them taste even better.

Air Fryer Chocolate Brownie Cookies

- Preparation Time: 15 minutes
- Cooking Time: 8-10 minutes
- Total Time: 25 minutes
- Serving Size: 12-14 cookies

Nutrition Facts (per serving, serving size: 1 cookie):

- Calories: 200
- Fat: 11g
- Protein: 3g
- Fiber: 1g

Ingredients:

- Unsalted butter, melted: 1/2 cup
- Granulated sugar: 1/2 cup
- Brown sugar: 1/2 cup
- Large eggs: 2
- Vanilla extract: 1 teaspoon
- All-purpose flour: 1 cup
- Unsweetened cocoa powder: 1/2 cup
- Baking powder: 1/2 teaspoon
- Salt: 1/4 teaspoon
- Semisweet chocolate chips: 1 cup

Instructions:

- Put the air fryer into preheating mode and set the temperature to 350°F (175°C) for 5 minutes.
- In a bowl for mixing, combine the melted butter, white sugar, and brown sugar by whisking them together until thoroughly mixed.
- Add eggs and vanilla extract Continue whisking until the mixture is smooth.
- Mix the all-purpose flour, cocoa powder, baking powder, and salt together in a separate mixing bowl by combining all of the ingredients together in the same way.
- While stirring constantly, gradually add the dry ingredients to the liquid component bowl. Stir until everything is thoroughly blended.
- Mix in the little chocolate bars.
- Put the cookie dough into a greased air fryer basket or tray, being sure to leave about 2 inches of space between each ball of dough.
- Put the basket or tray into the air fryer and set the timer for 8 to 10 minutes, or until the cookies are

firm outside but remain somewhat pliable in the middle.
- Take the basket or tray out of the air fryer and wait a few minutes for the cookies to cool down before attempting to remove them from the air fryer.

Variations:

- To give the cookie dough a satisfying crunch, stir in a half cup of finely chopped nuts, such as pecans or walnuts.
- Substitute white or peanut butter chips for the semisweet chocolate chips to create a different flavor.

Air Fryer Blackberry Cobbler:

- Preparation Time: 15 minutes
- Cooking Time: 20-25 minutes
- Total Time: 35-40 minutes
- Serving Size: 4-6 servings

Nutrition Facts (per serving):

- Calories: 220
- Fat: 8g
- Protein: 2g
- Fiber: 3g

Ingredients:

- Fresh blackberries: 2 cups
- Granulated sugar: 1/2 cup
- All-purpose flour: 1/2 cup
- Baking powder: 1/2 teaspoon
- Baking soda: 1/4 teaspoon
- Salt: 1/4 teaspoon
- Milk: 1/2 cup
- Unsalted butter, melted: 1/4 cup
- Vanilla extract: 1 teaspoon

Instructions:

- Put the air fryer into preheating mode and set the temperature to 350°F (175°C) for 5 minutes.
- Mix blackberries and 1/4 cup granulated sugar in a bowl.
- In a separate bowl, whisk flour, the remaining 1/4 cup of granulated sugar, baking powder, baking soda, and salt.
- Keep stirring as you add milk, melted butter, and vanilla to the dry ingredients. Fully combine everything by whisking.
- Place the blackberries in a ramekin or dish suitable for an air fryer and butter it. Spread the blackberries out in equal layers.
- Place the batter on top of the blackberries, then use a spoon to smooth it into an equal layer.
- Put the dish or ramekin into the air fryer and cook for 20 to 25 minutes, or until the cobbler is golden brown and a toothpick inserted into the center comes out clean.

- Take the dish or ramekin out of the air fryer and allow the cobbler to cool for a few minutes before serving.

Variations:

- Replace blackberries with blueberries, raspberries, or strawberries.
- Add 1/4 teaspoon of cinnamon to the batter for a homey taste.
- Top cobbler with vanilla ice cream or whipped cream.

Air Fryer Sweet Potato Fries with Maple Syrup

- Preparation Time: 10 minutes
- Cooking Time: 15-20 minutes
- Total Time: 25-30 minutes
- Serving Size: 4 servings

Nutrition Facts (per serving):

- Calories: 180
- Fat: 7g
- Protein: 1g
- Fiber: 3g

Ingredients:

- Medium sweet potatoes: 2, peeled and cut into fries
- Olive oil: 2 tablespoons
- Salt: 1/2 teaspoon
- Black pepper: 1/4 teaspoon
- Maple syrup: 1/4 cup
- Unsalted butter: 1 tablespoon

Instructions:

- Put the air fryer into preheating mode and set the temperature to 350°F (175°C) for 5 minutes.
- To prepare the sweet potato fries, combine the sweet potatoes, olive oil, salt, and black pepper in a large mixing bowl.
- Place the seasoned potato fries in the basket of the air fryer and spread them out so that they are in a single layer.
- Cook the fries for 15-20 minutes, turning halfway, until crispy and golden brown.
- Melt butter in a small pot and stir in maple syrup until fully incorporated.
- Take the fries out of the air fryer's basket, and drizzle the maple syrup mixture all over the fries.

- Serve the fries as soon as possible while they are piping hot and crisp.

Variations:

- For an additional layer of flavor, sprinkle some cinnamon on top of the fries.

Air Fryer Baked Peaches

- Preparation Time: 10 minutes
- Cooking Time: 12-15 minutes
- Total Time: 22-25 minutes
- Serving Size: 4 servings

Nutrition Facts (per serving):

- Calories: 120
- Fat: 7g
- Protein: 1g
- Fiber: 2g

Ingredients:

- Ripe peaches: 4
- Unsalted butter, melted: 2 tablespoons
- Honey: 2 tablespoons
- Ground cinnamon: 1/4 teaspoon
- Ground nutmeg: 1/4 teaspoon
- Salt: 1/4 teaspoon
- Chopped pecans: 1/4 cup

Instructions:

- Put the air fryer into preheating mode and set the temperature to 375°F (190°C) for 5 minutes.
- To prepare the peaches, cut them in half lengthwise and carefully remove the pits from each half.
- Mix melted butter, honey, cinnamon, nutmeg, and salt in a bowl.
- Apply the mixture with a pastry brush to the cut side of each peach half, coating them uniformly.
- Put cut-side-up peaches in the air fryer basket and top with chopped pecans.
- Cook the peaches in an air fryer for 12 to 15 minutes or until they reach the desired consistency of being tender and caramelized.

- After a few minutes, remove the peaches from the air fryer basket and let them cool for a while before serving.

Variations:

- Dessert is cooked peaches with vanilla ice cream or whipped cream.
- Replace pecans with walnuts or almonds.
- Before air-frying, sprinkle brown sugar on the peaches to caramelize them.

Air Fryer Blueberry Lemon Cake

- Preparation Time: 15 minutes
- Cooking Time: 25-30 minutes
- Total Time: 40-45 minutes
- Serving Size: 8 servings

Nutrition Facts (per serving):

- Calories: 250
- Fat: 12g
- Protein: 4g
- Fiber: 2g

Ingredients:

- All-purpose flour: 1 1/2 cups
- Granulated sugar: 1/2 cup
- Unsalted butter, melted: 1/2 cup
- Eggs: 2
- Milk: 1/2 cup
- Baking powder: 1 tablespoon
- Salt: 1/2 teaspoon
- Lemon zest: 1 tablespoon
- Fresh blueberries: 1 cup

Instructions:

- Put the air fryer into preheating mode and set the temperature to 325°F (165°C) for 5 minutes.
- Combine the flour, sugar, baking powder, salt, and lemon zest in a mixing bowl for a perfectly blended batter. Whisk to mix everything.
- Add the melted butter with eggs and milk in a mixing bowl until everything is well mixed.
- Add the fresh blueberries to the mixture.
- Spray a 7-inch cake pan with cooking spray and pour the batter inside.
- Put the cake pan inside the air fryer.
- Set the air fryer to 25-30 minutes and start cooking.

- To Know whether the cake is ready, insert a toothpick into the middle of the cake; if the toothpick comes out clean, the cake is ready.
- Wait a few minutes until the cake cools before serving.

Variations:

- Add a tablespoon of lemon juice to the batter for an extra lemon taste.
- Replace blueberries with raspberries, blackberries, or strawberries.
- Whipped cream and fresh lemon zest top the cake.

Air Fryer Chocolate Pudding

- Preparation Time: 5 minutes
- Cooking Time: 10 minutes
- Chilling Time: 1-2 hours
- Total Time: 1 hour, 15 minutes
- Serving Size: 4 servings

Nutrition Facts (per serving):

- Calories: 220
- Fat: 8g
- Protein: 5g
- Fiber: 3g

Ingredients:

- Granulated sugar: 1/2 cup
- Unsweetened cocoa powder: 1/3 cup
- Cornstarch: 1/4 cup
- Salt: 1/4 teaspoon
- Whole milk: 2 cups
- Vanilla extract: 1 teaspoon
- Semisweet chocolate chips: 1/4 cup

Instructions:

- Put the sugar, cocoa powder, cornstarch, and salt into a bowl and mix them together until the mixture is completely smooth.
- Add the milk slowly while stirring the mixture until it is completely smooth.
- Mix in some chocolate chips, along with some vanilla extract.
- In a heat-resistant bowl that fits in your air fryer basket, place the mixture.
- Put the bowl in the air fryer basket, and set the temperature to 350°F (or 175°C) for ten minutes.

- After 10 minutes, remove the bowl from the air fryer and let the pudding cool.
- Place the bowl in the refrigerator for one to two hours, covered with plastic wrap, until the pudding has reached the desired consistency.

Variations:

- Spice up chocolate pudding with cinnamon or cayenne pepper.
- Serve pudding with whipped cream, nuts, or berries.

Air Fryer Apple Cider Donuts

- Preparation Time: 15 minutes
- Cooking Time: 6-8 minutes per batch
- Total Time: 30-35 minutes
- Serving Size: 12 donuts

Nutrition Facts (per donut):

- Calories: 150
- Fat: 5g
- Protein: 2g
- Fiber: 1g

Ingredients:-

For the Donuts:-
- All-purpose flour: 2 cups
- Granulated sugar: 1/2 cup
- Baking powder: 1 tablespoon
- Baking soda: 1/2 teaspoon
- Salt: 1/2 teaspoon
- Ground cinnamon: 1/2 teaspoon
- Ground nutmeg: 1/4 teaspoon
- Eggs: 2
- Apple cider: 1/2 cup
- Milk: 1/4 cup
- Unsalted butter, melted: 2 tablespoons

- Vanilla extract: 1 teaspoon

For the Topping:

- Unsalted butter, melted: 1/4 cup
- Granulated sugar: 1/2 cup
- Ground cinnamon: 2 teaspoons

Instructions:-

- Put the air fryer into preheating mode and set the temperature to 350°F (175°C) for 5 minutes.
- Start by grabbing two mixing bowls.
- In one, combine the flour, sugar, baking powder, baking soda, salt, cinnamon, and nutmeg.
- In the other, whisk together the eggs, apple cider, milk, melted butter, and vanilla extract. Ensure that all ingredients are evenly mixed.
- Then add the liquid ingredients to the dry ones and stir until well combined.
- Put the batter in a piping bag or a zip-top bag with one of the corners cut off to use as a piping bag.

- To perfectly prepare your air fryer donuts, carefully pipe the batter into each mold of your donut pan, filling them about 2/3rd.
- Put the cake pan inside the air fryer.
- Set the air fryer to 6-8 minutes and start cooking until it is golden brown and a toothpick put into the center comes out clean.
- Brush the doughnuts with the melted butter, then roll them in the cinnamon sugar coating while the donuts are still warm.
- Serve the doughnuts warm.

Variations:

- For a more nuanced flavor, stir one teaspoon of apple pie spice into the batter before baking.
- Apple sauce or apple juice can be used in place of apple cider.
- Drizzle some caramel or maple glaze over the donuts for a sweeter treat.

Air Fryer Scones:

- Preparation Time: 15 minutes
- Cooking Time: 10-12 minutes per batch
- Total Time: 30-35 minutes
- Serving Size: 8 scones

Nutrition Facts (per scone):

- Calories: 220
- Fat: 10g
- Protein: 4g
- Fiber: 1g

Ingredients:

- All-purpose flour: 2 cups
- Granulated sugar: 1/4 cup
- Baking powder: 1 tablespoon
- Baking soda: 1/2 teaspoon
- Salt: 1/2 teaspoon
- Unsalted butter, cold and cut into small pieces: 1/2 cup
- Buttermilk: 2/3 cup
- Large egg: 1
- Vanilla extract: 1 teaspoon

Instructions:

- Put the air fryer into preheating mode and set the temperature to 350°F (175°C) for 5 minutes.
- Mix sugar, flour, baking soda, baking powder, and salt in a bowl. Whisk together until evenly mixed.
- Place the butter in the bowl, and then, using your fingers or a pastry blender, incorporate the butter into the flour mixture until the mixture resembles coarse crumbs.
- Whisk together the buttermilk, egg, and vanilla extract in a separate dish. Set this mixture aside.
- Mix the dry and liquid ingredients until they are almost completely combined.
- After letting the dough rest for a short while, move it onto a lightly floured surface. Form a ball by kneading the dough several times.
- Now Form a circle using the dough that is approximately 1 inch thick.
- Cut the dough into eight equal wedges and place them on a piece of parchment paper cut to the size of the air fryer basket.

- Put the scones and parchment paper in the air fryer basket.
- Place cake pan in air fryer. Turn the air fryer on for 10-12 minutes until golden brown and crispy. A toothpick inserted into the middle comes out clean.
- Served warm with jam or clotted cream.

Variations:

- Add 1/2 cup of dried cranberries, raisins, or currants to the dough.
- For a heartier texture, replace half the all-purpose flour with whole wheat.
- Add 1 teaspoon of your preferred spice, such as cinnamon or nutmeg, to flavor the dough.

Air Fryer Gingerbread Cookies:

- Total Time: 40 minutes
- Prep Time: 30 minutes
- Cook Time: 10 minutes
- Yield: 24 cookies

Nutrition Facts (per cookie):

- Calories: 90
- Fat: 4g
- Protein: 1g
- Fiber: 0g

Ingredients:

- All-purpose flour: 2 cups
- Baking soda: 1 teaspoon
- Salt: 1/2 teaspoon
- Ground ginger: 2 teaspoons
- Ground cinnamon: 1 teaspoon
- Ground cloves: 1/4 teaspoon
- Ground nutmeg: 1/4 teaspoon
- Unsalted butter, at room temperature: 1/2 cup
- Granulated sugar: 1/2 cup
- Molasses: 1/2 cup
- Large egg: 1
- Vanilla extract: 1 teaspoon
- Powdered sugar for dusting (optional)

Instructions:

- Put the air fryer into preheating mode and set the temperature to 350°F (175°C) for 5 minutes.
- Mix flour, salt, ginger, cinnamon, cloves, nutmeg, and baking soda in a large bowl.
- Now, mix butter and sugar together in separate bowls. Make the mixture light and frothy using an electric mixer. Now, in this mixture, Add the molasses, egg, and vanilla extract. Again, beat together until everything is well combined.
- Gradually mix the dry and wet ingredients and stir until the cookie dough is smooth.
- Form the dough into a ball and then wrap it in a piece of plastic wrap to prevent it from drying out. Put it in the fridge and leave it for at least an hour so that the temperature can drop.
- To achieve the perfect consistency, gently roll out the chilled dough onto a floured surface until it reaches a thickness of approximately 1/4 inch.

- Using cookie cutters, create the required shapes, then set them in the air fryer, leaving some space between each one.
- Bake the cookies in the air fryer for 8 to 10 minutes or until the centers are set, and the edges have a light brown coloration.
- After cooking the cookies in an air fryer, take them out and set them on a wire rack to cool.
- Sprinkle some powdered sugar over the cookies. (Optional)

Variations:

- For an enhanced ginger taste and a coarser texture, the dough might benefit from the addition of a half cup's worth of chopped crystallized ginger.
- Frost and sprinkle biscuits made using different cookie cutters.

Air Fryer Caramelized Bananas:

- Preparation Time: 5 minutes
- Cooking Time: 10 minutes
- Servings: 4

Nutrition facts (per serving): 162 Cal (5g fat, 1g protein, 3g fiber)

Ingredients:

- Ripe bananas: 2
- Brown sugar: 1 tablespoon
- Butter: 1 tablespoon
- Cinnamon powder: 1 teaspoon
- Vanilla ice cream, to serve (optional)

Instructions:

- Put the air fryer into preheating mode and set the temperature to 350°F (175°C) for 5 minutes.
- Bananas should be peeled and cut into rounds with a thickness of about 14/16 of an inch.
- In a small bowl, combine the brown sugar and cinnamon powder.

- Melt the butter in a microwave-safe or stove-top bowl until it's smooth and liquid.
- First, coat each slice of banana in the melted butter, then roll it in the mixture of brown sugar and cinnamon.
- Put the banana slices coated in a single layer in the air fryer's basket.
- Bananas need around 7 minutes in an air fryer to get brown and caramelized.
- Serve the bananas as soon as possible, and if desired, top each serving with a dollop of vanilla ice cream.

Variations:

- Use vegan butter or coconut oil for a vegan variation.
- Add chopped walnuts or pecans to the brown sugar mixture for crunch and taste.
- Serve caramelized bananas without ice cream with whipped cream or caramel sauce.
- For a salty-sweet taste, sprinkle sea salt on bananas before eating.

Air Fryer Apple Turnovers

- Preparation Time: 15 minutes
- Cooking Time: 12-15 minutes
- Servings: 4

Nutrition facts (per serving): 348 Cal (19g fat, 3g protein, 3g fiber)

Ingredients:

- Puff pastry sheet, thawed: 1
- Medium-sized apples, peeled, cored, and diced: 2
- Brown sugar: 2 tablespoons
- Lemon juice: 1 tablespoon
- Cinnamon: 1/2 teaspoon
- Nutmeg: 1/4 teaspoon
- Unsalted butter: 1 tablespoon
- Egg, beaten: 1
- Water: 1 tablespoon
- Powdered sugar, for dusting

Instructions:

- Put the air fryer into preheating mode and set the temperature to 375°F (190°C) for 5 minutes.

- Melted The butter is in a saucepan over medium heat. Then, add the diced apples, brown sugar, lemon juice, cinnamon, and nutmeg.
- Cook for five to seven minutes, stirring the mixture regularly, until the sugar is completely dissolved and the apples are tender. Let it cool.
- On a lightly floured surface, unfold the puff pastry sheet and cut it into four equal squares.
- To prepare an egg wash, beat the egg with a little bit of water in a separate bowl.
- Scoop a spoonful of the apple mixture onto the center of each puff pastry square once it has cooled down.
- Use egg wash to brush the pastry's edges.
- Each pastry square should be folded in half to form a triangle, and then the edges should be pressed with a fork to seal.
- Apply a light coating of the remaining egg wash to the tops of the turnovers.

- Put the turnovers in the air fryer basket and cook them for 12 to 15 minutes or until they have puffed up and turned a golden brown.
- Remove the turnovers from the air fryer to cool. Before serving, dust the dish with powdered sugar.

Variations:

- Add one tablespoon of chopped nuts or raisins to give the apple filling more flavor and texture.
- Try substituting other kinds of fruit, like pears or peaches, for the apples in the recipe.
- Before serving, drizzle the turnovers with a glaze that combines powdered sugar and milk.

Air Fryer Oatmeal Raisin Cookies

- Preparation Time: 10 minutes
- Cooking Time: 10 minutes per batch
- Servings: 12 cookies

Nutrition facts (per cookie): 160 Cal (7g fat, 2g protein, 1g fiber)

Ingredients:

- Unsalted butter, softened: 1/2 cup
- Brown sugar: 1/2 cup
- Granulated sugar: 1/4 cup
- Egg: 1
- Vanilla extract: 1 teaspoon
- All-purpose flour: 1 cup

- Baking soda: 1/2 teaspoon
- Ground cinnamon: 1/2 teaspoon
- Salt: 1/4 teaspoon
- Old-fashioned rolled oats: 1 1/2 cups
- Raisins: 1/2 cup

Instructions:

- Put the air fryer into preheating mode and set the temperature to 350°F (175°C) for 5 minutes.
- Add butter and sugar and cream them together in bowls. Make the mixture light and frothy using an electric mixer. Now add the molasses, egg, and vanilla extract. Again, mix thoroughly.
- In a separate bowl, add cinnamon, salt, baking soda, and flour, combined with a light hand, and stir until smooth.
- Gradually mix the dry and wet ingredients and stir until the cookie dough is smooth.
- Now mix in the rolled oats as well as the raisins.
- Place rounded tablespoons of dough onto the air fryer, leaving about an inch of space between each one.

- Achieve perfect golden-brown crispy cookies by air-frying them one batch at a time for 10 minutes.
- Take the cookies out of the air fryer and place them on a cooling rack to cool down.

Variations:

- If you want your cookies to have a bit more crunch and flavor, chop some nuts, like walnuts or pecans, and add them to the dough for the cookies.
- Replace the raisins with chopped dates or dried cranberries.
- Instead of butter, use coconut oil and whole wheat flour.

Air Fryer Mini Fruit Pies

- Preparation Time: 15 minutes
- Cooking Time: 10-12 minutes
- Servings: 6 mini pies

Nutrition facts (per mini pie): 225 Cal (11g fat, 2g protein, 1g fiber)

Ingredients:

- Refrigerated pie dough: 1 sheet
- Fruit jam or preserves (such as strawberry or raspberry): 1/2 cup
- Fresh fruit (such as blueberries or sliced strawberries): 1/4 cup
- Cornstarch: 1 tablespoon
- Lemon juice: 1 tablespoon
- Egg, beaten: 1

- Powdered sugar, for dusting

Instructions:

- Put the air fryer into preheating mode and set the temperature to 375°F (190°C) for 5 minutes.
- Unroll the pie dough onto a lightly floured surface. Make six circles out of the dough by cutting it with a round cutter around four inches in diameter.
- In a small bowl, combine the fresh fruit, jam or preserves made from fruit, cornstarch, and lemon juice, and stir well to combine the ingredients.
- Add a spoonful of fruit mixture to each pie dough circle.
- Create a rustic pie shape by folding the dough's edges over the fruit filling. To seal, press the edges together.
- Use the beaten egg to glaze the pies.
- Put the pies in the air fryer basket and cook them for 10 to 12 minutes, or until the crust is browned golden and the filling is bubbling.

- Remove the pies from the air fryer and set them aside to cool. Serve with a dusting of powdered sugar.

Variations:

- Make the filling with various fruits, such as peaches, blackberries, or cherries, each with a unique flavor.
- For an additional layer of flavor, consider sprinkling the fruit filling with some cinnamon or nutmeg.

Air Fryer Coconut Macaroons

- Preparation Time: 10 minutes
- Cooking Time: 8-10 minutes per batch
- Servings: 12 macaroons

Nutrition facts (per macaroon): 124 Cal (6g fat, 2g protein, 1g fiber)

Ingredients:

- Large egg whites: 2
- Granulated sugar: 1/4 cup
- Vanilla extract: 1/2 teaspoon
- Salt: 1/4 teaspoon
- Sweetened shredded coconut: 1 1/2 cups
- Sweetened condensed milk: 2/3 cup

Instructions:

- Put the air fryer into preheating mode and set the temperature to 350°F (175°C) for 5 minutes.
- In a medium bowl, beat the egg whites until they are foamy
- Add granulated sugar, sweetened condensed milk, vanilla extract, and salt to the bowl, and whisk the ingredients thoroughly.
- Now add and mix the shredded coconut into the egg white mixture until it is evenly coated with the egg whites.
- Form coconut balls with a spoon or cookie scoop. Place on a parchment-lined plate.
- Prepare the air fryer basket with frying spray or parchment paper. Place the macaroons in the basket with space between them. You may need to air cook them in batches, depending on the size of your air fryer.

- Air Fry the macaroons for eight to ten minutes or until they reach a color between light gold and golden brown.
- Once they have finished cooking in the air fryer, take the macaroons from the appliance and let them cool on a wire rack.

Variations:

- Stir in some finely chopped nuts, like almonds or pecans, to give the coconut mixture more crunch and flavor.
- Replace sweetened shredded coconut with unsweetened for a less sweet macaroon.

Air Fryer Chocolate Hazelnut Cake

- Preparation Time: 15 minutes
- Cooking Time: 20-25 minutes
- Servings: 6-8

Nutrition facts (per serving): 215 Cal (11g fat, 3g protein, 2g fiber)

Ingredients:

- All-purpose flour: 1/2 cup
- Granulated sugar: 1/2 cup
- Unsweetened cocoa powder: 1/4 cup
- Baking powder: 1/2 teaspoon
- Baking soda: 1/4 teaspoon
- Salt: 1/4 teaspoon
- Vegetable oil: 1/4 cup

- Hazelnut spread (such as Nutella): 1/4 cup
- Large egg: 1
- Hot water: 1/2 cup
- Powdered sugar, for dusting (optional)

Instructions:

- Put the air fryer into preheating mode and set the temperature to 350°F (175°C) for 5 minutes.
- In a large mixing bowl, whisk together sugar, flour, baking powder, baking soda, cocoa powder, and salt.
- In a separate bowl, use a whisk to combine the egg, hazelnut spread, and vegetable oil until smooth.
- Gradually mix the dry and wet ingredients and stir until well combined.
- Add the hot water in a slow, steady stream while constantly stirring the mixture until it is lump-free and smooth.
- Grease a 6-inch round cake pan, pour batter in, and smooth the top with a spatula.
- Place the cake pan inside the air fryer.

- Set the air fryer to 20-25 minutes and start cooking until golden brown, a toothpick is inserted into the middle, and it comes out clean.
- After taking the cake from the air fryer and allowing it to cool for a few minutes, remove it from the pan and place it on a wire rack to finish cooling entirely.

Variations:

- For an additional layer of flavor and texture, garnish the cake with shaved chocolate or chopped hazelnuts.
- If you want a spread with a different flavor, try substituting peanut butter or almond butter for the hazelnut spread.

Air Fryer Funnel Cake

- Preparation Time: 15 minutes
- Cooking Time: 8-10 minutes per batch
- Servings: 4

Nutrition facts (per serving): 318 Cal (8g fat, 6g protein, 1g fiber)

Ingredients:

- All-purpose flour: 1 cup
- Baking powder: 1 teaspoon
- Salt: 1/4 teaspoon
- Granulated sugar: 1/4 cup
- Large egg: 1
- Milk: 1/2 cup
- Vanilla extract: 1/2 teaspoon

- Vegetable oil, for frying
- Powdered sugar, for dusting

Instructions:

- Whisk the flour, baking powder, salt, and sugar together in a large bowl.
- Mix the egg, milk, and vanilla extract separately, whisking the ingredients together.
- Gradually mix them and stir until the cookie dough is smooth. Stir the mixture until it is entirely smooth and free of lumps.
- Put the batter in a big bag with a zip-top and make a hole in one corner of the bag using a pair of scissors.
- Put the air fryer into preheating mode and set the temperature to 350°F (175°C) for 5 minutes.
- Coat the air fryer basket with a very thin layer of vegetable oil to prepare it.
- Create a spiral pattern on the greased basket of the air fryer by piping the batter over the surface in a circular manner. Be cautious about making overlaps in the batter to end up with a solid cake.

- Bake the cake in an air fryer for about eight to ten minutes or until it has a golden brown color and a crispy texture.
- Use tongs to carefully transfer the cake to a paper towel-lined plate to absorb excess oil.
- Add powdered sugar to the funnel cake before serving.

Variations:

- Add whipped cream and fresh berries to the funnel cake for a delicious touch.
- For an autumn treat, add cinnamon or pumpkin spice to the batter.
- For added pleasure, drizzle funnel cake with chocolate or caramel sauce.

Air Fryer Pumpkin Spice Donuts

- Preparation Time: 20 minutes
- Cooking Time: 8-10 minutes per batch
- Servings: 6-8

Nutrition facts (per serving): 206 Cal (8g fat, 3g protein, 1g fiber)

Ingredients:

- All-purpose flour: 1 cup
- Granulated sugar: 1/2 cup
- Baking powder: 1 teaspoon
- Baking soda: 1/4 teaspoon
- Salt: 1/4 teaspoon
- Pumpkin spice: 1 teaspoon
- Canned pumpkin puree: 1/2 cup
- Large egg: 1

- Milk: 1/4 cup
- Vegetable oil: 1/4 cup
- Vanilla extract: 1 teaspoon
- Powdered sugar for dusting

Instructions:

- Whisk flour, sugar, baking soda, baking powder, pumpkin pie spice, and salt in a large bowl.
- Combine the pumpkin puree, egg, milk, vegetable oil, and vanilla extract in a separate dish and whisk until smooth.
- Gradually mix the dry and wet ingredients, and stir until the cookie dough is smooth. Stir the mixture until it is entirely smooth and free of lumps.
- Put the air fryer into preheating mode and set the temperature to 350°F (175°C) for 5 minutes.
- Spray a doughnut pan with cooking spray to prevent sticking.
- Put the batter in a large bag with a zip-top and make a hole in one corner of the bag using a pair of scissors.

- Pipe the batter into the oiled doughnut pan, filling each shape approximately 2/3 full.
- Put the donut pan in the basket of the air fryer and air fry the donuts for 8 to 10 minutes or until golden brown and thoroughly cooked.
- To remove the donuts from the air fryer basket carefully, use tongs and then place them on a wire rack to cool.
- Before serving, sprinkle the funnel cake with powdered sugar.

Variations:

- Drizzle melted chocolate or caramel sauce over the donuts for an extra decadent treat.
- For a unique take on this classic dish, try substituting apple or chai spice for the pumpkin pie spice.

Air Fryer Chocolate Caramel Brownies

- Preparation Time: 15 minutes
- Cooking Time: 20-25 minutes
- Servings: 9

Nutrition facts (per serving): 300 Cal (15g fat, 4g protein, 1g fiber)

Ingredients:

- Unsalted butter, melted: 1/2 cup
- Granulated sugar: 1 cup
- Unsweetened cocoa powder: 1/2 cup
- Salt: 1/2 teaspoon
- Baking powder: 1/2 teaspoon
- Large eggs: 2
- Vanilla extract: 1 teaspoon
- All-purpose flour: 1/2 cup
- Caramel sauce: 1/2 cup
- Powdered sugar, for dusting

Instructions:

- Melt the butter and add sugar, cocoa powder, salt, and baking powder in a large mixing bowl Whisk them properly.

- Another bowl Whisk the eggs and vanilla essence until the batter is completely smooth.
- Add the flour gradually and stir until it is just combined.
- Mix the dry ingredients into the wet components until the brownie batter is smooth and completely integrated.
- Spray some nonstick cooking spray on a square baking dish.
- Toss half the brownie mix into the prepared baking dish.
- Drizzle the caramel sauce over the batter and spread it out evenly.
- The last of the batter should be poured on top of the caramel layer, and then it should be smoothed out using a spatula.
- Put the air fryer into preheating mode and set the temperature to 350°F (175°C) for 5 minutes.
- Put the baking dish into the basket of the air fryer, and air fry the brownies for 20 to 25 minutes, or until they have reached the desired consistency and a

- toothpick inserted into the center of the pan comes out clean.
- After carefully removing the baking dish from the air fryer basket with tongs, wait for it to cool for a few minutes before continuing.
- Before serving, sprinkle powdered sugar over the brownies.

Variations:

- Add chocolate chips or chopped nuts to give the brownie batter more flavor and texture.
- Before serving, drizzle some additional caramel sauce over the top of the brownies.

Air Fryer Mixed Berry Crisp

- Preparation Time: 20 minutes
- Cooking Time: 15-20 minutes
- Servings: 4-6

Nutrition facts (per serving): 247 Cal (8g fat, 3g protein, 4g fiber)

Ingredients:

- Mixed berries (such as blueberries, raspberries, and blackberries): 2 cups
- Granulated sugar: 2 tablespoons
- Cornstarch: 1 tablespoon
- All-purpose flour: 1/2 cup
- Old-fashioned oats: 1/2 cup
- Light brown sugar: 1/2 cup
- Salt: 1/4 teaspoon

- Ground cinnamon: 1/2 teaspoon
- Unsalted butter, softened: 1/4 cup

Instructions:

- Mix the berries with the granulated sugar and cornstarch in a large bowl until they are evenly covered with the sugar and starch.
- Place the berry mixture in an air fryer-compatible oiled baking dish.
- Mix flour, oats, brown sugar, salt, and cinnamon in another bowl.
- Add softened butter to the mixer and use your fingertips or a pastry cutter until it forms a crumbly dough. Now sprinkle the oat mixture over the top of the berry mixture until it is completely covered.
- Put the air fryer into preheating mode and set the temperature to 375°F (190°C) for 5 minutes.
- Place the baking dish in the air fryer's basket and bake for 15 to 20 minutes until the berry mixture is bubbling and the topping is golden and crisp.
- Let it cool for a few minutes after air-frying.

- If preferred, serve the mixed berry crisp warm with vanilla ice cream or whipped cream.

Variations:

- You can use your preferred fruit combination in place of the mixed berries, such as peaches and blueberries or apples and cranberries.
- Add chopped nuts or shredded coconut to give the oat topping more flavor and texture.

Air Fryer Peanut Butter Fudge

- Preparation Time: 5 minutes
- Cooking Time: 10 minutes
- Chilling Time: 2-4 hours
- Servings: 16

Nutrition facts (per serving): 239 Cal (15g fat, 5g protein, 1g fiber)

Ingredients:

- Creamy peanut butter: 1 cup
- Unsalted butter: 1/2 cup
- Salt: 1/4 teaspoon
- Vanilla extract: 1 teaspoon
- Powdered sugar: 3 cups

Instructions:

- Combine the peanut butter, unsalted butter, salt, and vanilla extract in a sizable mixing bowl.
- Microwave the mixture on high for one to two minutes or until the butter has melted and the mixture is smooth.
- To the mixture, add the powdered sugar, and stir it until the sugar is completely incorporated and the mixture is smooth.
- Spray some nonstick cooking spray on a square baking dish that will fit inside your air fryer and set it aside.
- Put the peanut butter fudge mixture in the greased dish and spread it evenly.
- Put the air fryer into preheating mode and set the temperature to 350°F (175°C) for 5 minutes.
- Insert the baking dish into the air fryer basket and set the timer for 10 minutes.
- Remove the baking dish from the basket with tongs and let it cool for a few minutes before serving.

- Place the dish in the refrigerator for 2 to 4 hours, or until the fudge has reached the desired consistency, and cover it with plastic wrap.
- After the fudge has been chilled for the appropriate amount of time, cut it into 16 squares using a sharp knife.

Variations:

- Add chopped peanuts or chocolate chips to the fudge for texture and taste.
- Almond or cashew butter tastes different from peanut butter.
- Serve fudge pieces drizzled with melted chocolate.

Air Fryer Sweet Potato Casserole

- Preparation Time: 15 minutes
- Cooking Time: 35 minutes
- Servings: 4-6

Nutrition facts (per serving): 298 Cal (12g fat, 3g protein, 4g fiber)

Ingredients:

- Large sweet potatoes, peeled and chopped: 4
- Unsalted butter, softened: 1/4 cup
- Brown sugar: 1/4 cup
- Milk: 1/4 cup
- Ground cinnamon: 1/2 teaspoon
- Ground nutmeg: 1/4 teaspoon

- Salt: 1/4 teaspoon
- Mini marshmallows: 1 cup
- Chopped pecans: 1/2 cup

Instructions:

- Set the air fryer to preheat at 350°F (175°C) for 5 minutes.
- In a large bowl, mix chopped sweet potatoes, melted butter, brown sugar, milk, cinnamon, nutmeg, and salt.
- Mix the ingredients using a potato masher or an electric mixer until everything is well combined and the sweet potatoes are mashed.
- Next, place the sweet potato mixture in a greased air fryer baking dish.
- Set your air fryer to 375°F and air fry the sweet potato mixture for 20-25 minutes, or until the edges are lightly browned and the sweet potatoes are tender.

- While the sweet potatoes are cooking, mix mini marshmallows and the chopped pecans together in a small mixing dish.
- After the sweet potatoes are cooked in the air fryer, sprinkle the marshmallow and pecan mixture over the sweet potatoes.
- Place the baking dish back into the air fryer and continue to air fry for 10 to 15 minutes, or until the marshmallows have puffed up and turned golden brown.
- After carefully removing the baking dish from the air fryer basket with tongs, wait for it to cool for a few minutes before continuing.
- Serve the sweet potato casserole warm with your favorite main course as a side dish.

Variations:

- Add one tablespoon of maple syrup or honey to increase the sweetness of the sweet potato mixture.
- For a savory twist, sprinkle chopped bacon over the sweet potato casserole.

Air Fryer Blueberry Lemon Bars

- Preparation Time: 15 minutes
- Cooking Time: 25 minutes
- Chilling Time: 2 hours
- Servings: 8-10

Nutrition facts (per serving): 248 Cal (11g fat, 3g protein, 1g fiber)

Ingredients:

- Unsalted butter, softened: 1/2 cup
- Granulated sugar: 1/4 cup
- All-purpose flour: 1 cup
- Salt: 1/4 teaspoon

For the Lemon Blueberry Filling:

- Large eggs: 2
- Granulated sugar: 1/2 cup
- All-purpose flour: 1/4 cup
- Fresh lemon juice: 1/4 cup
- Lemon zest: 1 tablespoon
- Fresh blueberries: 1 cup

Instructions:

- To make the frosting, put the softened butter in a large mixing bowl along with a quarter cup of granulated sugar. Combine all ingredients in a mixing bowl and beat them until they are airy and frothy.
- After adding 1 cup of all-purpose Flour and 1/4 teaspoon of salt, the butter mixture is thoroughly combined.
- Apply the mixture evenly to the bottom of a greased square baking dish in your air fryer.
- In a separate bowl, whisk the eggs, half a cup of granulated sugar, a quarter cup of all-purpose flour, lemon juice, and lemon zest until thoroughly combined and smooth.
- Add the blueberries to the mixture using a folding motion.
- Pour the blueberry-lemon mixture over the crust in the baking dish and evenly distribute it with a spatula.
- Put the air fryer into preheating mode and set the temperature to 350°F (175°C) for 5 minutes.

- Put the baking dish in the air fryer basket for 20 to 25 minutes, or until the blueberry lemon mixture is set and the edges are golden brown.
- After carefully removing the baking dish from the air fryer basket with tongs, wait for it to cool for a few minutes before continuing.
- Cover the dish with plastic wrap and refrigerate for at least two hours to firm up the blueberry lemon bars.
- After the bars have been refrigerated appropriately, cut them into 8 to 10 equal squares using a sharp knife.
- Serve the blueberry lemon bars chilled, and store any leftovers in the refrigerator.

Variations:

- For a flavor that's a little bit different, try substituting some raspberries or strawberries for the blueberries.
- Add one tablespoon of corn flour to the blueberry-lemon mixture for a thicker consistency.
- Before serving, drizzle some powdered sugar glaze over the bars.

Air Fryer Cinnamon Sugar Pretzels:

- Preparation Time: 10 minutes
- Cooking Time: 8-10 minutes
- Servings: 4

Nutrition facts (per serving): 275 Cal (9g fat, 3g protein, 1g fiber)

Ingredients:

- Refrigerated pizza dough: 1 can
- Unsalted butter, melted: 2 tablespoons
- Granulated sugar: 1/4 cup
- Ground cinnamon: 1 tablespoon

Instructions:

- Put the air fryer into preheating mode and set the temperature to 375°F (190°C) for 5 minutes.
- Lightly dust a flat surface with flour. Then, gently roll out your refrigerated pizza dough onto the surface until it's uniformly thin. Using a sharp knife or pizza cutter, slice the dough into strips approximately 1/2 inch wide.
- Transform each strip of dough into a mesmerizing pretzel shape and carefully lay them on a generously greased air fryer tray.

- Next, apply a layer of melted butter to each pretzel, ensuring every inch of dough is perfectly coated.
- Stir the ground cinnamon with the granulated sugar in a small bowl.
- Evenly distribute the cinnamon sugar mixture throughout the surface of the pretzels.
- Cook the seasoned pretzels in an air fryer set to 350°F for 8 to 10 minutes or until golden brown.
- Use tongs to remove the tray from the basket and transfer the pretzels to a plate.
- Serve after a few minutes of cooling.

Variations:

- Spice up the cinnamon sugar mixture with nutmeg or allspice to try new flavors.
- Warm caramel sauce should be served alongside the pretzels for dipping.
- If you want the cinnamon sugar mixture to have a crunchier texture, add some finely chopped nuts, such as pecans or almonds.

Air Fryer Chocolate Covered Cherries:

- Preparation Time: 10 minutes
- Cooking Time: 5-7 minutes
- Servings: 4

Nutrition facts (per serving): 156 Cal (10g fat, 2g protein, 3g fiber)

Ingredients:

- Fresh cherries, pitted: 1 cup
- Semisweet chocolate chips: 1/2 cup
- Coconut oil: 1 tablespoon
- Chopped almonds or other nuts (optional): 1/4 cup

Instructions:

- Rinse and dry cherries to prepare them. Remove all stems and pits.
- Chocolate chips and coconut oil melt together in a microwave or on the stovetop in a small basin that serves as a mixing bowl. Combine well by stirring.
- Coat each cherry well in the melted chocolate by dipping them individually. Lift the cherry with a fork and tilt it so any extra chocolate runs off.
- Place All the chocolate-covered cherries on a greased air fryer tray.
- If you so choose, you can dust the top of each cherry with finely chopped almonds or other types of nuts.
- Cook in the air fryer for 5 to 7 minutes or until the chocolate has reached the desired consistency.
- Using tongs, remove the food from the basket of the air fryer, and then wait a few minutes for it to cool down before serving.

Variations:

- If you want a different flavor, try substituting milk chocolate or white chocolate chips for semisweet chocolate chips.
- To decorate chocolate-covered cherries, drizzle melted chocolate in a different color.

Air Fryer Strawberry Shortcake:

- Preparation Time: 10 minutes
- Cooking Time: 10 minutes
- Servings: 4

Nutrition facts (per serving): 299 Cal (12g fat, 4g protein, 2g fiber)

Ingredients:

- Fresh strawberries, hulled and sliced: 1 pound
- Granulated sugar: 1/4 cup
- All-purpose flour: 1 1/2 cups
- Baking powder: 2 teaspoons
- Salt: 1/4 teaspoon
- Unsalted butter, chilled and cubed: 1/4 cup
- Milk: 1/2 cup
- Heavy cream: 1 tablespoon
- Whipped cream for topping

Instructions:

- Put the air fryer into preheating mode and set the temperature to 375°F (190°C) for 5 minutes.

- Mix fresh sliced strawberries with granulated sugar in a small bowl. Leave the mixture for 10 minutes to macerate and sweeten.
- Mix salt, baking powder, and all-purpose flour in a large bowl.
- Mix the cold butter cut into cubes into the flour using a pastry cutter or your hands until the mixture becomes crumbly.
- Stir in the milk until it is almost completely mixed.
- Place the dough on a lightly dusted surface with flour and gently knead it until it forms a ball.
- Roll out the dough to a thickness of about 1/2 inch and cut out circles with a biscuit cutter or the rim of a drinking glass.
- Use heavy cream to paint the tops of the dough circles.
- Put the dough rounds in the air fryer basket and cook them for 8 to 10 minutes or until golden brown.
- After making the macerated strawberries, split the shortcakes in half.

- Spoon the strawberries and their juices over the bottom half of the shortcake, add whipped cream on top, and finish by placing the other half of the shortcake on top.

Variations:

- If you want to change the flavor of the shortcake, try adding a teaspoon of vanilla extract or some lemon zest to the dough.
- Instead of strawberries, mix in fresh berries like blueberries and raspberries.
- For an extra tangy kick, drizzle some balsamic glaze over the strawberries that have been macerated.

Air Fryer Oreo Churros:

- Preparation Time: 10 minutes
- Cooking Time: 15 minutes
- Servings: 4

Nutrition facts (per serving): 266 Cal (14g fat, 5g protein, 1g fiber)

Ingredients:

- Water: 1 cup
- Unsalted butter: 2 tablespoons
- Granulated sugar: 1 tablespoon
- Salt: 1/4 teaspoon
- All-purpose flour: 1 cup
- Eggs: 2
- Vanilla extract: 1/2 teaspoon
- Finely crushed Oreo cookies: 1/2 cup
- Granulated sugar: 1/4 cup
- Ground cinnamon: 1 teaspoon
- Cooking spray

Instructions:

- Put the air fryer into preheating mode and set the temperature to 350°F (175°C) for 5 minutes.

- Over medium heat, combine the water, butter, granulated sugar, and salt in a medium saucepan. Boil the mixture thoroughly.
- Next, reduce the heat to low and add all-purpose flour while stirring vigorously with a wooden spoon. Continue this process until the dough comes together in a ball and pulls away from the sides of the pan.
- Once you have finished, ensure the heat is turned off and allow the mixture to cool for a few minutes.
- Add eggs and vanilla extract to the flour mixture, stirring the ingredients until evenly spread.
- Add the Oreo cookies that have been finely crushed.
- In a small bowl, mix the granulated sugar and ground cinnamon. Stirring until well blended.
- Apply some cooking spray to the air fryer's basket.
- Put the churro batter in a piping bag with a star-shaped tip.
- Making 4-inch strips, pipe the churro ingredients into the air fryer basket.
- Prepare the churros in an air fryer for 10 to 12 minutes or until golden.

- After removing them from the air fryer, coat them with cinnamon and sugar.
- Serve warm with chocolate sauce or whipped cream.

Variations:

- Replace Oreos with chocolate chip or peanut butter cookies.
- Spike the cinnamon sugar with cayenne pepper or chili powder.

Air Fryer Peach Hand Pies:

- Preparation Time: 20 minutes
- Cooking Time: 12-15 minutes
- Servings: 4

Nutrition facts (per serving): 391 Cal (19g fat, 5g protein, 2g fiber)

Ingredients:

For the Pie Crust:

- All-purpose flour: 1 and 1/2 cups
- Salt: 1/4 teaspoon
- Unsalted butter, cold and cut into small cubes: 1/2 cup
- Ice-cold water: 3-4 tablespoons

For the Peach Filling:

- Diced peaches: 2 cups
- Granulated sugar: 1/4 cup
- Cornstarch: 1 tablespoon
- Cinnamon: 1/2 teaspoon
- Nutmeg: 1/4 teaspoon

- Vanilla extract: 1/2 teaspoon

For Assembly:

- Egg, beaten: 1
- Turbinado sugar: 1 tablespoon

Instructions:

- Preheat the air fryer to 375°F (190°C) for 5 minutes.
- Whisk all-purpose flour and salt in a large bowl.
- Place the cold butter cubes in the bowl and chop them into the flour with a pastry cutter or fork until the mixture resembles gritty sand.
- Mix while gradually including the ice-cold water, one spoonful at a time, to bring the dough together.
- Roll the dough to 1/8-inch thickness on a floured surface.
- Using a circular cookie cutter or a bowl as a guide, cut the dough into circles four inches in diameter.

- Combined diced peaches, granulated sugar, cornflour, cinnamon, nutmeg, and vanilla extract are in a separate bowl.
- Spread around one to two teaspoons' worth of the peach filling onto the bottom half of each dough circle.
- Place the filling in the center of the dough, cover it with the other half, and crimp the sides using a fork.
- Beat the egg and brush it over the tops of the pies, then sprinkle them with turbinado sugar.
- Spray some cooking spray over the basket of the air fryer.
- Place the pies in the air fryer's basket in a single layer, ensuring that they do not contact one another.
- Air fry the pies for 12–15 minutes until the crust is golden brown and the filling boils, whichever comes first.
- After air-frying, let the pies cool for a few minutes before serving.

Variations:

- Try substituting other kinds of fruit, like apples or berries, for the peaches in the recipe.
- To enhance the flavor of the peach filling, try adding a little bit of ground ginger or cardamom.

Air Fryer Caramel Popcorn

- Preparation time: 10 minutes
- Cooking time: 20 minutes
- Servings: 4

Nutrition facts (per serving): 222 Cal (10g fat, 1g protein, 1g fiber)

Ingredients:

- Popcorn kernels: 1/2 cup
- Unsalted butter: 1/4 cup
- Brown sugar: 1/2 cup
- Corn syrup: 1/4 cup
- Salt: 1/2 teaspoon
- Vanilla extract: 1/2 teaspoon

- Baking soda: 1/4 teaspoon

Instructions:

- Put the air fryer into preheating mode and set the temperature to 350°F (175°C) for 5 minutes.
- Pop the popcorn in an air popper or a covered pot on the stove.
- Melt butter in a saucepan over medium heat.
- Add the brown sugar, corn syrup, and salt to the saucepan, and stir the ingredients until they are completely incorporated.
- Cook the caramel mixture over medium heat, stirring it frequently, for approximately five to six minutes or until it thickens and turns a rich amber color.
- Mix the vanilla extract and baking soda in a bowl after taking the pan off the heat.
- After pouring the caramel mixture over the popcorn, give it a thorough toss so that the popcorn is covered in the caramel mixture evenly.
- One layer of caramelized popcorn in the air fryer basket.

- Cook the popcorn in the air fryer for 10 minutes, stirring every three to four minutes to ensure it cooks evenly.
- Cool the air-fried popcorn for a few minutes before serving.

Variations:

- Add some nuts, such as peanuts or almonds, that have been coarsely chopped for a little more crunch.
- For a taste that is equal parts sweet and salty, sprinkle a little bit of sea salt over the caramel popcorn.

Air Fryer Lemon Ricotta Cake:

- Preparation time: 15 minutes
- Cooking time: 25 minutes
- Servings: 6

Nutrition facts (per serving): 228 Cal (12g fat, 6g protein, 1g fiber)

Ingredients:

- All-purpose flour: 1/2 cup
- Almond flour: 1/4 cup
- Granulated sugar: 1/4 cup
- Baking powder: 1/2 teaspoon
- Baking soda: 1/4 teaspoon
- Salt: 1/8 teaspoon
- Ricotta cheese: 1/2 cup
- Unsalted butter, softened: 1/4 cup
- Egg: 1
- Lemon juice: 2 tablespoons
- Lemon zest: 1 teaspoon
- Vanilla extract: 1/2 teaspoon
- Powdered sugar for dusting (optional)

Instructions:

- Put the air fryer into preheating mode and set the temperature to 320 °F (160 °C) for 5 minutes.
- In a large bowl, mix all-purpose flour, almond flour, granulated sugar, baking powder, baking soda, and salt for the best texture and flavor. Whisk until well mixed.
- Whip melted ricotta and butter in a separate bowl until smooth.
- Add the egg, lemon juice, lemon zest, and vanilla extract to the ricotta mixture and beat everything until well combined.
- Gradually mix the dry and wet ingredients and stir until the cookie dough is smooth.
- After greasing a round cake pan with a diameter of 6 inches, pour the cake batter into the prepared pan.
- Place the cake pan in the air fryer.
- Bake it for 25 minutes, or if you stick a toothpick into the cake's center, it comes out clean.
- Take the cake out of the air fryer and let it cool for five to ten minutes in the pan before serving.

- After it has cooled for a while, gently take the cake from the pan and place it on a wire rack so that it may finish cooling.
- After the cake has had time to cool, you may dust it with powdered sugar and serve it.

Variations

- Add whipped cream and fresh berries to the cooled cake for a festive appearance.
- Orange ricotta cake uses orange juice and zest instead of lemon.
- Add 1/4 cup chopped nuts, like pistachios or almonds, to the cake batter for crunch.

Air Fryer Blackberry Bread:

- Preparation time: 15 minutes
- Cooking time: 40-45 minutes
- Servings: 8

Nutrition facts (per serving): 290 Cal (12g fat, 5g protein, 2g fiber)

Ingredients:

- All-purpose flour: 2 cups
- Baking powder: 1 teaspoon
- Baking soda: 1/2 teaspoon
- Salt: 1/2 teaspoon
- Unsalted butter, softened: 1/2 cup
- Granulated sugar: 1 cup
- Eggs: 2
- Vanilla extract: 1 teaspoon
- Milk: 1/2 cup
- Fresh blackberries: 1 cup

Instructions:

- Put the air fryer into preheating mode and set the temperature to 320°F (160°C) for 5 minutes.

- Mix all-purpose flour, baking powder, baking soda, and salt in a bowl.
- In a separate dish, beat the softened butter and granulated sugar until frothy.
- Add the vanilla essence and mix well. After that, add the eggs one at a time, mixing well between each addition.
- Alternating with the milk, gradually add the dry components to the wet ones and mix until just blended.
- Mix in the fresh blackberries slowly.
- Put the mixture into a 7x2.5-inch oiled loaf pan.
- Put the cake pan in the air fryer.
- Bake it for 40 to 45 minutes, or if you stick a toothpick into the cake's center, it comes out clean.
- Take the cake out of the air fryer and let it cool for 5 to 10 minutes in the pan before serving.
- After it has cooled for a while, gently take the cake from the pan and place it on a wire rack so that it may finish cooling.
- **Slice and serve.**

Variations:

- Raspberries, blueberries, or a combination of berries can be used instead of blackberries.
- Drizzle powdered sugar and lemon juice over the cooled bread for a sweet-tart finish.

Air Fryer Chocolate Peanut Butter Cups:

- Preparation time: 10 minutes
- Cooking time: 5-7 minutes
- Servings: 12

Nutrition facts (per serving): 136 Cal (10g fat, 3g protein, 1g fiber)

Ingredients:

- Semi-sweet chocolate chips: 1 cup
- Creamy peanut butter: 1/4 cup
- Coconut oil: 1 tablespoon
- Salt: 1/4 teaspoon
- Powdered sugar: 1/4 cup
- Creamy peanut butter: 1/4 cup
- Vanilla extract: 1/2 teaspoon

Instructions:

- Put the air fryer into preheating mode and set the temperature to 350°F (175°C) for 5 minutes.
- Combine the semi-sweet chocolate chips, 1/4 cup of creamy peanut butter, coconut oil, and salt in a microwave-safe bowl. Melt the mixture in intervals of

30 seconds, stirring between each melting session, until the liquid is entirely smooth.
- In another bowl, powdered sugar, 1/4 cup creamy peanut butter, and vanilla extract were mixed until smooth.
- Melt chocolate and put some in the bottom of silicone muffin cups.
- Add a small teaspoon of peanut butter mixture onto the cups' chocolate layer
- On top of the peanut butter mixture, spread another tablespoon's worth of the melted chocolate mixture.
- Air-fried the muffins for 7 minutes, or until the chocolate is set, with the muffin pan in the air fryer's basket.
- Remove the muffin tin from the air fryer and let it cool down.
- You may now serve the chocolate peanut butter cups by carefully removing them from the muffin tin.

Variations:

- Use milk or dark chocolate instead of semi-sweet.
- Replace the peanut butter with hazelnut spread or almond butter.
- On top of the chocolate layer, sprinkle some crushed peanuts or a light coating of sea salt for an additional textural and flavor component.

Air Fryer Mini Cheesecakes:

- Preparation time: 20 minutes
- Cooking time: 15 minutes
- Serving size: 4

Nutrition facts (per serving): 415 Cal (32g fat, 6g protein, 1g fiber)

Ingredients:

- Graham cracker crumbs - 1 cup
- Unsalted butter melted - 4 tbsp
- Cream cheese, softened - 8 oz
- Granulated sugar - 1/4 cup
- Vanilla extract - 1 tsp
- Eggs - 1 large
- Fresh lemon juice - 1 tbsp
- Whipped cream, for garnish
- Fresh berries, for garnish

Instructions:

- Put the air fryer into preheating mode and set the temperature to 350°F (175°C) for 5 minutes.
- Melt butter and graham cracker crumbs in a bowl and mix well.

- After lining a muffin tray, put 1 spoonful of graham cracker mixture in each liner. Pack silicone cupcake liners with a mixture of pressure.
- In a separate dish, use an electric mixer to whip the cream cheese until it is smooth.
- Continue beating the mixture after adding the sugar, vanilla extract, egg, and lemon juice to get a creamy and smooth consistency.
- Fill the cupcake liners approximately 3/4 with the cheesecake batter using a scoop.
- Place the liner into the air fryer at 350°F (175°C) for 15 minutes.
- When finished, take the air fryer liners out and let them cool for a while.
- After cooling, put them in the fridge for an hour.
- Chill and top with whipped cream and fruit.
- Toss with some whipped cream and fresh fruit, then refrigerate before serving.

Variations:

- Mix cream cheese, pumpkin pie spice, and 1/2 cup canned pumpkin puree.
- Blueberry compote, created by boiling fresh blueberries with sugar and lemon juice until thick, may be used as a cheesecake topping.
- Combine crushed Oreos with the Graham cracker crumbs to make a cookie and cream crust.

Air Fryer Strawberry Jam Thumbprint Cookies:

- Preparation time: 15 minutes
- Cooking time: 8-10 minutes
- Serving size: 4

Nutrition facts (per serving): 410 Cal (24g fat, 4g protein, 1g

Ingredients:

- All-purpose flour - 1 cup
- Unsalted Butter - 1/2 cup at room temperature
- Granulated sugar - 1/3 cup
- Salt - 1/4 tsp
- Egg yolk - 1 large
- Vanilla extract - 1 tsp
- Strawberry jam - 1/2 cup

Instructions:

- Mix flour and salt. Put aside.
- In a separate bowl, beat butter and sugar until fluffy and light.
- Add egg yolk and vanilla extract to the butter mixture and mix well.

- Mix the flour and butter and blend slowly and gradually until a dough is formed.
- The dough should be rolled into balls approximately the size of a tablespoon, and then the balls should be left aside.
- Use the palm of your hand to gently press down on each ball until it is the size of a small disc.
- Create a hollow in the centre of each biscuit by pressing your thumb or small spoon into the dough.
- Spread some strawberry jam. Fill in the space.
- Paced cookies in the basket of the air fryer.
- Bake at 350°F for 8-10 minutes until the edges are lightly golden.
- Let the cookies cool on a wire rack before serving.

Variations:

- Any jam or preserve can replace strawberry jam.
- Use holiday-themed jams to decorate the cookies.
- Add chopped nuts or chocolate chips to the dough for texture and taste.

Air Fryer Chocolate Chip Banana Bread:

- Preparation time: 15 minutes
- Cooking time: 40-45 minutes
- Serving size: 1 loaf (8-10 slices)

Nutrition facts (per serving): 286 Cal (13g fat, 4g protein, 2g fiber)

Ingredients:

- Ripe bananas: 3
- Unsalted butter, melted: 1/2 cup
- Granulated sugar: 1/2 cup
- Large eggs: 2
- Vanilla extract: 1 tsp
- All-purpose flour: 1 1/2 cups
- Baking powder: 1 tsp
- Baking soda: 1/2 tsp
- Salt: 1/2 tsp
- Chocolate chips: 1/2 cup

Instructions:

- Set the air fryer to preheat at 320°F (160°C) for 5 minutes.
- Mashing bananas with a fork in a large bowl makes them smooth.

- In a separate dish, mix the melted butter with sugar, eggs, and vanilla extract. Completely mix the ingredients.
- Combine the dry ingredients of baking soda, baking powder, and salt in a separate dish.
- Gently whisk the dry ingredients into the banana mixture. Avoid overmixing to ensure the perfect texture.
- Add some chocolate chips.
- Spray cooking spray into a loaf or cake pan, approximately a 7-inch.
- Spread the mixture on the pan carefully and distribute it all over the pan
- Put the cake pan into the air fryer.
- Set the air fryer to 30-35 minutes and start cooking.
- The cake is done when a toothpick inserted into its center comes out clean.
- After it has finished cooking, take the bread out of the air fryer and allow it to cool for ten minutes before slicing it and serving it.

Variations:

- Add chopped nuts, like walnuts or pecans, if you want more texture and crunch.
- You may substitute white chocolate chips or dried fruit like raisins or cranberries for the chocolate chips in this recipe.
- Add a teaspoon of cinnamon or nutmeg for a warm and comforting taste.

Air Fryer Banana Foster:

- Preparation time: 5 minutes
- Cooking time: 10 minutes
- Serving size: 4

Nutrition facts (per serving): 355 Cal (19g fat, 2g protein, 2g fiber)

Ingredients:

- Ripe bananas, sliced: 4
- Unsalted butter: 4 tablespoons
- Packed brown sugar: 1/2 cup
- Ground cinnamon: 1 teaspoon
- Dark rum: 1/4 cup
- Heavy cream: 1/4 cup
- Vanilla ice cream, for serving

Instructions:

- Put the air fryer into preheating mode and set the temperature to 350°F (175°C) for 5 minutes.
- Combine the sliced bananas, brown sugar, and cinnamon in a large bowl.

- Melt butter in a small saucepan on low to medium heat. After the butter has melted, pour in the rum and stir it together until it is completely incorporated.
- Pour the butter-rum mixture over the banana mixture, coating it evenly.
- Add the banana mixture to the air fryer basket and cook for 10 minutes. Make sure to give it a good toss halfway through to ensure even cooking.
- While the bananas are cooking, put the heavy cream in a small saucepan and place it over medium heat. Stir it frequently until it reaches a gentle simmer, and then set it aside.
- After the bananas have finished cooking, place them in a serving bowl, and then pour the warmed heavy cream over the top of the bananas.

- Warm the banana foster made in the air fryer and serve it with a dollop of vanilla ice cream on top.

Variations:

- Add 1/2 cup chopped pecans or walnuts to the banana mixture before cooking for a nutty flavor.
- Replace the rum with 1/4 cup of orange juice or apple cider to make it kid-friendly.
- Instead of bananas, try sliced apples or peaches.

Air Fryer Pumpkin Pie Bites:

- Preparation Time: 10 minutes
- Cooking Time: 8-10 minutes
- Servings: 4

Nutrition facts (per serving): 280 Cal (14g fat, 4g protein, 1g fiber)

Ingredients:

- Pumpkin puree: 1/2 cup
- Brown sugar: 1/4 cup
- Egg: 1
- Ground cinnamon: 1/2 teaspoon
- Ground ginger: 1/4 teaspoon
- Ground cloves: 1/8 teaspoon
- Salt: 1/8 teaspoon
- Heavy cream: 1/4 cup
- Refrigerated pie crust (1 package)
- Granulated sugar: 1 tablespoon
- Whipped cream for serving (optional)

Instructions:

- Add pumpkin puree, brown sugar, egg, cinnamon, ginger, cloves, salt, and heavy cream to a mixing bowl to prepare the pumpkin mixture. Mix thoroughly.

- On a surface that has been dusted with flour, roll out your pie dough until it is of a thickness that is appropriate for making hand pies.
- To make the circles, use a circular cookie cutter to cut out the rolled-out dough in a size that is approximately 2 to 3 inches in diameter. To make a total of 12 circles, reroll any dough scraps that are left over as necessary.
- Place around a tablespoon of the pumpkin mixture in the center of each circle.
- Sprinkle some granulated sugar in each circle on top of the pumpkin mixture.
- Place the circles in the air fryer's basket while ensuring they do not contact one another.
- Fry in an air fryer at a temperature of 350°F for 8 to 10 minutes or until the crust is golden brown and the filling is set.
- If preferred, serve with whipped cream on the side.

Variations:

- Increase cinnamon, ginger, and cloves in the filling for more spice.
- Add nutmeg or allspice to the filling for a richer taste.

Air Fryer Cinnamon Apple Fritters:

- Preparation time: 15 minutes
- Cooking time: 8 minutes
- Serving size: 4

Nutrition facts (per serving): 284 Cal (2g fat, 6g protein, 1g fiber)

Ingredients:

- All-purpose flour - 1 cup
- Baking powder - 1 tsp
- Cinnamon powder - 1 tsp
- Salt - 1/4 tsp
- Brown sugar - 1/4 cup
- Milk - 1/2 cup
- Egg - 1
- Vanilla extract - 1 tsp
- Apples (peeled and chopped) - 1 cup
- Powdered sugar - 1/4 cup

Instructions:

- Put the air fryer into preheating mode and set the temperature to 350°F (175°C) for 5 minutes.
- Mix flour, baking powder, cinnamon, salt, and brown sugar in a bowl.

- Whisk the egg, vanilla extract, and milk together in a separate bowl until all ingredients are combined.
- Add the dry ingredients to the wet mixture, and stir everything together very well until it is completely combined.
- Before moving on to the next step, add the apple chunks to the batter.
- Before using the air fryer, liberally coat the basket with cooking spray. This will prevent food from sticking to the basket and make clean-up much simpler.
- Put the mixture in the air fryer basket one tablespoon at a time, leaving adequate space between each one.
- Air-fry the fritters for 6–8 minutes until golden brown and crispy.
- As soon as they are ready, take the fritters out of the air fryer and set them on a wire rack to cool.
- Before serving, sprinkle with powdered sugar to finish.

Variations:

- For more spice, add 1/4 teaspoon powdered nutmeg and ginger to the dry ingredients.
- 1/4 cup chopped walnuts or pecans give crunch.
- Add vanilla ice cream or whipped cream.

Air Fryer Chocolate Donuts:

- Preparation time: 10 minutes
- Cooking time: 8-10 minutes
- Servings: 6 donuts

Nutrition facts (per serving): 204 Cal (8g fat, 4g protein, 1g fiber)

Ingredients:

For the Cake:

- All-purpose flour: 1/2 cup
- Granulated sugar: 1/4 cup
- Unsweetened cocoa powder: 1/4 cup
- Baking powder: 1/2 teaspoon
- Baking soda: 1/4 teaspoon
- Salt: 1/4 teaspoon
- Buttermilk: 1/2 cup
- Large egg: 1
- Unsalted butter, melted: 2 tablespoons
- Vanilla extract: 1/2 teaspoon
- Cooking spray

For the Glaze:

- Powdered sugar: 1/2 cup
- Unsweetened cocoa powder: 2 tablespoons
- Milk: 2-3 tablespoons
- Vanilla extract: 1/4 teaspoon

Instructions:

- Pre-heat the air fryer at 350°F (175°C) for 5 minutes.
- Mix the flour, sugar, cocoa powder, baking powder, baking soda, and salt in a large bowl until well blended.
- In a separate bowl, combine the egg, the melted butter, the buttermilk, and the vanilla extract by whisking the ingredients together.
- Gently pour the wet ingredients into the dry ones and whisk to make the batter.
- Spray air fryer molds with cooking spray.
- Carefully fill each mold 3/4 full of batter for perfectly baked muffins.
- When ready, place the molds in an air fryer basket and cook for 8-10 minutes. Insert a toothpick in the center to check if it is cooked through - a clean toothpick indicates that it is ready to be served.
- Remove the donuts from the air fryer after a few minutes and let them cool before removing them.

- To prepare the glaze, obtain a small mixing bowl and combine the powdered sugar, cocoa powder, milk, and vanilla extract by whisking them together.
- After the donuts have cooled, run the tops through the glaze and lay them aside for a few minutes to enable the glaze to harden.
- Serve and enjoy!

Variation:

- For taste and texture, sprinkle chopped nuts, coconut flakes, or chocolate chips on the glaze.

Air Fryer Caramelized Pineapple

- Preparation Time: 10 minutes
- Cooking Time: 10-12 minutes
- Servings: 4

Nutrition facts (per serving): 136 Cal (7g fat, 1g protein, 1g fiber)

Ingredients:

- Ripe pineapple, peeled, cored, and cut into chunks: 1
- Brown sugar: 1/4 cup
- Unsalted butter, melted: 1/4 cup
- Vanilla extract: 1 tsp
- Pinch of salt

Instructions:

- Set the air fryer to preheat at 400°F (195°C) for 5 minutes.
- Brown sugar, melted butter, vanilla essence, and a pinch of salt are mixed in a small bowl until everything is evenly mixed.
- Now, add the pineapple pieces to the bowl, and toss them to coat them equally with the brown sugar mixture.

- Place pineapple chunks in air fryer basket in a single layer.
- Fry the pineapple in an air fryer for 10 to 12 minutes, or until it has a caramelized and golden brown appearance, turning it over halfway through the cooking time.
- Serve hot caramelized pineapple immediately.

Variations:

- To add warmth and spice, sprinkle cinnamon powder over pineapple pieces before air-frying.
- Add rum or coconut rum to the brown sugar mixture to make this dish boozier.
- Caramelized pineapple on vanilla ice cream or Greek yogurt is a healthy dessert.

Air Fryer Maple Glazed Donut Holes

- Preparation time: 10 minutes
- Cooking time: 8 minutes
- Serving size: 4

Nutrition facts (per serving): 375 Cal (12g fat, 5g protein, 1g fiber)

Ingredients:

- All-purpose flour - 1 cup
- Baking powder - 1 tsp
- Salt - 1/4 tsp
- Milk - 1/2 cup
- Egg - 1
- Melted butter - 1/4 cup
- Sugar - 1/2 cup
- Cinnamon powder - 1 tsp
- Maple syrup - 1/4 cup
- Powdered sugar - 1/4 cup

Instructions:

- Mix flour, baking powder, and salt in a bowl using a spoon.
- In a separate bowl, mix Milk, eggs, and melted butter

- Combine the wet and dry ingredients in a mixing bowl until it forms a soft dough.
- Form the dough into small balls about the size of a golf ball.
- Put the balls of dough into the basket of the air fryer, leaving some room between each one so they can cook evenly.
- Air-fried the doughnut holes at 350°F (175°C) for 6 to 8 minutes or until golden brown and cooked through.
- While baking doughnut holes, Put sugar and cinnamon powder in a small bowl.
- Make a glaze in a separate dish by combining the maple syrup and powdered sugar and whisking them together until smooth.
- When the doughnut holes are made, dunk them in the cinnamon-sugar mixture and let the sugar adhere.
- Spread the maple glaze over the top of the doughnut holes
- Serve warm.

Variations:

- Use chocolate or caramel glaze on doughnut holes instead of maple.
- Sprinkle sea salt on doughnut holes before dripping the glaze for a sweet-salty taste.

Air Fryer Lemon Curd Tartlets

- Preparation time: 15 minutes
- Cooking time: 10 minutes
- Servings: 4

Nutrition facts (per serving): 205 Cal (13g fat, 1g protein, 1g fiber)

Ingredients:

For the Pastry:

- All-purpose flour: 1/2 cup
- Unsalted butter, cubed and chilled: 1/4 cup
- Ice water: 1/8 cup

For the Filling:

- Lemon curd: 1/4 cup
- Powdered sugar: 1 tablespoon

Instructions:

- Mix the flour and butter together in a bowl of a suitable size. Stir together until it resembles coarse crumbs.

- Add the ice water very slowly while continuing to stir the mixture until it forms a ball. Put the dough in a plastic bag, then into the refrigerator for about a quarter of an hour.
- Set the air fryer to preheat at 350°F (175°C) for 5 minutes.
- Roll the dough out to a thickness of 1/8 of an inch on a surface that has been dusted lightly with flour only lightly. Cut circles of dough slightly larger than silicone cupcake liners with a cookie cutter or drinking glass.
- Press the dough circles into the cupcake liners' bottoms and sides.
- Put lemon curd in each cupcake liner.
- air fryer for eight to ten minutes, until the crust is golden and the lemon curd has set.
- After cooling in the air fryer for a few minutes, remove the tartlets from the silicone liners.
- Sprinkle confectioners' sugar on tartlets before serving.

Variations:

- Add a few drops of yellow food colouring to the lemon curd to make the tartlets brighter.
- Top the tartlets with whipped cream or a dollop of meringue for added sweetness.
- Substitute the lemon curd for lime or orange curd for a different citrus flavor.

Air Fryer Peach Melba:

- Preparation time: 10 minutes
- Cooking time: 15 minutes
- Serving size: 4

Nutrition facts (per serving): 234 Cal (5g fat, 3g protein, 5g fiber)

Ingredients:

- Peaches, pitted and sliced: 2
- Raspberries: 1 cup
- Sugar: 1/4 cup
- Water: 1/4 cup
- Vanilla extract: 1/2 tsp
- Vanilla ice cream: 2 cups

Instructions:

- Pre-heat the air fryer at 350°F (175°C) for 5 minutes.
- Cut peaches and raspberries and mix in a bowl.
- Mix sugar and water in a small saucepan. Continue whisking over medium heat until sugar dissolves.
- To add the perfect finishing touch, remove the saucepan from the heat and gently mix in the vanilla extract until fully incorporated.

- Pour the sugar syrup over the fruit mixture and stir to combine.
- Place the fruit mixture in an air fryer-safe baking dish or basket.
- Air-fry the fruit for 10 to 12 minutes or until the fruit is tender and the juices are bubbling, whichever comes first.
- Take the fruit combination from the air fryer and let it cool for a few minutes.
- Divide the fruit mixture evenly among four serving bowls.
- Serve immediately, adding a scoop of vanilla ice cream to the top of each bowl before doing so.

Variations:

- Replace raspberries with strawberries or blackberries.
- Replace vanilla ice cream with whipped cream or Greek yogurt.

Air Fryer Cherry Clafoutis

- Preparation time: 10 minutes
- Cooking time: 20 minutes
- Servings: 4

Nutrition facts (per serving): 267 Cal (4g fat, 9g protein, 1g fiber)

Ingredients:

- Fresh cherries, pitted: 2 cups
- Eggs: 3
- Granulated sugar: 1/2 cup
- All-purpose flour: 1/2 cup
- Milk: 1 cup
- Vanilla extract: 1 tsp
- Salt: 1/4 tsp
- Powdered sugar, for dusting

Instructions:

- Wash and pit cherries. Leave them whole or halve as desired.
- Pre-heat your air fryer at 350°F (175°C) for 5 minutes.
- In a bowl, combine the eggs and the granulated sugar.
- Add all-purpose flour slowly while whisking to avoid lumps.

- Mix in milk, vanilla, and a pinch of salt. Blend the batter until lump-free.
- Prepare your air fryer by greasing a cake pan or oven-safe dish in the shape of a round that will fit inside the basket.
- Place pitted cherries evenly in the greased dish.
- Cover cherries evenly with batter.
- Put the cherry-batter dish in the preheated air fryer.
- Air fry the clafoutis for 25–30 minutes at 350°F (175°C).
- Clafoutis is done when set in the center and golden brown on top.
- Allow the cherry clafoutis to cool after air-frying.
- Serve the clafoutis with powdered sugar on top, if desired.
- Serve warm air-fried cherry clafoutis. The traditional serving temperature is room temperature or slightly warm.

Variations:

- Peaches, plums, and berries can replace fresh cherries.
- Before cooking, add a spoonful of cherry liqueur or kirsch.

Air Fryer Chai Spiced Rice Pudding

- Preparation Time: 5 minutes
- Cooking Time: 25 minutes
- Servings: 4

Nutrition facts (per serving): 182 Cal (3g fat, 4g protein, 1g fiber)

Ingredients:

- Cooked rice: 1 cup
- Milk: 1 1/2 cups
- Sugar: 1/4 cup
- Salt: 1/4 tsp
- Cinnamon stick: 1
- Cardamom pods: 2
- Ground ginger: 1/4 tsp
- Ground cloves: 1/4 tsp
- Ground nutmeg: 1/4 tsp
- Raisins: 1/4 cup
- Whipped cream and cinnamon powder, for serving (optional)

Instructions:

- Mix the cooked rice with the milk, sugar, and salt in a large bowl. Mix together effectively.

- Add the cinnamon stick, cardamom pods, ginger, cloves, and nutmeg to the mixture and stir.
- Add the raisins and thoroughly combine everything.
- The mixture is poured into the air fryer suitable baking dish and then placed within the air fryer basket.
- Cook the rice in an air fryer at 350°F (175°C) for 20 to 25 minutes or until the pudding has reached the desired consistency.
- After removing it from the air fryer, wait a few minutes to cool down.
- Before serving, if you choose to, top each portion with some whipped cream and a dusting of cinnamon spice.

Variations:

- Half-and-half or heavy cream instead of milk makes it creamier.
- Add chopped almonds or pecans for texture and crunch.

Air Fryer Mixed Berry Galette:

- Preparation time: 20 minutes
- Cooking time: 15-20 minutes
- Servings: 4

Nutrition facts (per serving): 226 Cal (11g fat, 3g protein, 2g fiber)

Ingredients:

- Mixed berries (strawberries, blueberries, raspberries, and blackberries): 1 cup
- Granulated sugar: 2 tablespoons
- Cornstarch: 1 tablespoon
- Lemon juice: 1 teaspoon
- Vanilla extract: 1/2 teaspoon

- Puff pastry sheet, thawed: 1
- Egg, beaten: 1
- Coarse sugar for sprinkling
- Whipped cream or ice cream, for serving

Instructions:

- Put the air fryer into preheating mode and set the temperature to 375°F (190°C) for 5 minutes.
- In a dish of medium size, mix together the blueberries, blackberries, raspberries, and strawberries with the granulated sugar, cornstarch, lemon juice, and vanilla extract. Combine all of the ingredients in such a way that the berries are fully submerged in the mixture.
- Roll out the puff pastry on a surface dusted with flour into a circle approximately 8 inches (20 cm) in diameter.
- Transfer the puff pastry onto a piece of parchment paper.
- Spoon the berry mixture onto the center of the puff pastry, leaving a 2-inch (5 cm) border around the edges.

- After placing the berries in the center of the puff pastry, fold the dough's sides over them and crimp the four corners together.
- To finish, give the edges a light coating of beaten egg and generously sprinkle them with coarse sugar.
- Slide the parchment paper with the galette onto the air fryer basket.
- Cook the galette in an air fryer for fifteen to twenty minutes, or until the crust is golden brown and the berries are bubbling, whichever occurs first.
- The galette should be allowed to cool after the parchment paper has been removed. Serve as a dessert with whipped cream or ice cream for a truly decadent experience.

Variations:

- Try using different fruits, such as peaches, apples, or pears, for the filling.
- Spice up the filling with cinnamon or nutmeg.
- Serve with a milk-and-powdered sugar glaze.

Air Fryer Chocolate Soufflé:

- Preparation time: 10 minutes
- Cooking time: 12 minutes
- Serving size: 2

Nutrition facts (per serving): 385 Cal (27g fat, 6g protein, 2g fiber)

Ingredients:

- Semisweet chocolate chips: 1/2 cup
- Unsalted butter: 2 tablespoons
- Granulated sugar: 1 tablespoon
- All-purpose flour: 1 tablespoon
- Vanilla extract: 1/4 tsp
- Large egg, separated
- Cream of tartar: 1/8 tsp
- Powdered sugar for dusting

Instructions:

- Pre-heat the air fryer at 350°F (175°C) for 5 minutes.
- Melt the chocolate chips and butter together in a microwave-safe bowl. Melt it in the microwave for 30 seconds at a time, stirring occasionally.
- Mix the flour, sugar, and vanilla extract in a separate dish and whisk until mixed.

- Whisk the egg yolk into the chocolate mixture until fully combined for a delicious chocolate taste. Stir in the dry ingredients until smooth.
- Take a different bowl and whisk the egg white with cream of tartar until it forms stiff peaks.
- Next, gently add the egg whites to the chocolate mixture. Take care not to over mix so as not to deflate the mixture. This technique will result in a perfect texture for your dish.
- After greasing two ramekins of 8 ounces each, divide the mixture so that each one receives an equal amount.
- Cook the ramekins for a total of 12 minutes after placing them in the air fryer.
- Take the soufflés out of the air fryer and let them cool for a few minutes before serving.
- Dusted with powdered sugar, this dish should be served right away.

Variations:

- Add 1/4 teaspoon ground cinnamon or cardamom to the dry ingredients for a spiced chocolate soufflé.
- If you want to make the soufflés into an even more luxurious dessert, you may top them with whipped cream or a dollop of ice cream.
- The texture and flavor of the final product can be improved by using chopped nuts or dried fruit in the batter.

Air Fryer Cinnamon Sugar Apple Rings

- Preparation Time: 10 minutes
- Cooking Time: 8 minutes
- Serving Size: 4

Nutrition facts (per serving): 197 Cal (2g fat, 4g protein, 3g fiber)

Ingredients:

- Medium-sized apples: 2
- Flour: 1/4 cup
- Cinnamon: 1 teaspoon
- Nutmeg: 1/4 teaspoon
- Salt: 1/4 teaspoon
- Milk: 1/2 cup
- Egg: 1
- Vanilla extract: 1 teaspoon
- Bread crumbs: 1/2 cup
- Granulated sugar: 1/4 cup
- Cinnamon: 1 teaspoon
- Cooking spray

Instructions:

- Put the air fryer into preheating mode and set the temperature to 370°F (187°C) for 5 minutes.

- Peel and slice the apples into thin 1/4-inch pieces to prepare them.
- Mix cinnamon, nutmeg, salt, and flour until well-blended.
- Combine milk, an egg that has been beaten, and some vanilla extract in a separate bowl. Use a whisk to mix everything until well combined.
- Dip each apple slice in the flour mixture, then the milk mixture, and then coat them in bread crumbs.
- Arrange apple slices in a single layer in the air fryer basket with room between them for uniform cooking. This prevents stickiness and sogginess.
- Spray the apple slices with a very thin coating of cooking spray.
- Fry the apple slices in the air fryer for 8 minutes, during which time they should be flipped over once.
- In a separate bowl, sugar and cinnamon are combined and stirred until uniform.
- To add some extra sweetness and flavor to the cooked apple slices, generously sprinkle the cinnamon sugar mixture on top right before serving.

Enjoy this delectable treat immediately while it's still hot.

Variations:

- Use cornflakes or cinnamon toast crunch instead of bread crumbs to cover apple slices.
- To make the coating sweeter, add one tablespoon of brown sugar to the combination of flour and salt.
- Apple slices, vanilla ice cream, or whipped cream can be combined to make a scrumptious dessert, which can then be brought to the table and enjoyed by the diners.

Air Fryer Peanut Butter and Jelly Donuts

- Preparation Time: 10 minutes
- Cooking Time: 6-8 minutes
- Serving Size: 4

Nutrition facts (per serving): 298 Cal (16g fat, 5g protein, 1g fiber)

Ingredients:

- Refrigerated biscuits: 1 can
- Creamy peanut butter: 4 tablespoons
- Your favorite jelly or jam: 4 tablespoons
- Powdered sugar: 1/4 cup
- Milk: 2 tablespoons
- Vanilla extract (optional): 1/2 teaspoon

Instructions:

- Pre-heat the air fryer at 350°F (175°C) for 5 minutes.
- Remove the biscuits from the can and break them up.
- Press or roll out each biscuit until it is around 1/4 inch thick.
- Mix peanut butter, vanilla, and powdered sugar in a small bowl. Whisk well until smooth.

- Spread 1 spoonful of peanut butter mixture and 1 tablespoon of jelly in the middle of each biscuit.
- After you've finished, carefully fold the biscuit in half and make sure the sides are well sealed.
- Put the filled biscuits in the air fryer basket and ensure they aren't stacked on top of each other.
- Fry the doughnuts for 6 to 8 minutes or until they have a golden brown color all the way through.
- To prepare the glaze, put the powdered sugar and milk into a small dish and mix them until they are entirely smooth.
- After the biscuits have cooled for a few minutes, drizzle the glaze over them.
- Serve the delicious, warm biscuits, and enjoy!

Variations:

- You can use any jam or jelly that strikes your fancy, whether grape, raspberry, or strawberry.
- Sprinkle chopped peanuts or banana slices on donuts to boost flavor.
- Add some cinnamon if you want the peanut butter and jelly mixture to taste even better.

Air Fryer Sweet Cornbread Muffins:

- Preparation time: 10 minutes
- Cooking time: 10 minutes
- Servings: 4

Nutrition facts (per serving): 416 Cal (18g fat, 8g protein, 2g fiber)

Ingredients:

- Yellow cornmeal: 1 cup
- All-purpose flour: 1 cup
- Granulated sugar: 1/4 cup
- Baking powder: 1 tablespoon
- Salt: 1/2 teaspoon
- Milk: 1/2 cup
- Sour cream: 1/2 cup
- Unsalted butter, melted: 1/4 cup
- Large eggs: 2

Instructions:

- Pre-heat the air fryer at 350°F (175°C) for 5 minutes.
- Mix cornmeal, flour, sugar, baking powder, and salt in a bowl. Whisk the ingredients well.

- Grab another bowl to prepare the wet ingredients, and gently whisk the milk, sour cream, melted butter, and eggs until fully combined.
- Gradually mix the dry and wet ingredients, and stir until smooth.
- Fill each lined muffin cup 3/4 full with mixture using a scoop.
- Cook the muffins in the air fryer basket for 10 to 12 minutes, until the tops are golden brown and a toothpick inserted into the center of one of the muffins comes out clean.
- Take the muffins out of the air fryer and let them rest for a few minutes before serving so that they can cool down.

Variations:

- Add shredded cheddar cheese or crumbled cooked bacon for flavor.
- Add honey butter or honey to the muffins for sweetness.

Air Fryer Apple Cinnamon Empanadas:

- Preparation time: 20 minutes
- Cooking time: 10 minutes
- Servings: 4

Nutrition facts (per serving): 255 Cal (14g fat, 2g protein, 2g fiber)

Ingredients:

- Refrigerated pie crust: 1
- Large apple, peeled and chopped: 1
- Lemon juice: 1 tablespoon
- Brown sugar: 1/4 cup
- Ground cinnamon: 1/4 teaspoon
- Unsalted butter, melted: 1 tablespoon
- Egg, beaten: 1
- Water: 1 tablespoon
- Granulated sugar for sprinkling

Instructions:

- Preheat the air fryer to 375°F (190°C) for 5 minutes.
- In a bowl, mix chopped apple, lemon juice, brown sugar, cinnamon, and melted butter. Blend the ingredients to make a tasty, fragrant mixture.
- To make the pie, lay out the dough and then cut it into four circles of equal size.

- Place approximately two teaspoons of the apple mixture in the middle of each circle.
- To seal the circle, simply fold it in half and press the edges together until they seal.
- Make a crimped edge on each empanada by pressing it with a fork.
- To create a delicious golden brown crust on your empanadas, stir an egg and water in a small bowl to make an egg wash.
- Generously brush the top of each empanada with the egg wash and then sprinkle with a pinch of granulated sugar.
- Place your filled empanadas in the basket of an air fryer and cook them for 8 to 10 minutes, or until they reach the desired level of crispiness and color.

Variations:

- Add a pinch of nutmeg or cloves to the apple mixture for extra flavor.
- Substitute pears or peaches for the apples.
- Drizzle caramel sauce over the empanadas before serving.

Air Fryer Lemon Pound Cake:

- Preparation time: 10 minutes
- Cooking time: 45 minutes
- Serving size: 4

Nutrition facts (per serving): 481 Cal (23g fat, 6g protein, 1g fiber)

Ingredients:

- All-purpose flour: 1 and 1/2 cups
- Baking powder: 1/2 teaspoon
- Baking soda: 1/2 teaspoon
- Salt: 1/4 teaspoon
- Unsalted butter, softened: 1/2 cup
- Granulated sugar: 3/4 cup
- Large eggs: 2
- Lemon juice: 1/4 cup
- Lemon zest: 2 teaspoons
- Whole milk: 1/2 cup

Instructions:

- Preheat the air fryer to 320°F (160°C) for 5 minutes.
- In a medium bowl, mix flour, baking powder, baking soda, and salt. To fully combine the ingredients, whisk them together.

- In another bowl, beat the butter and sugar until light and fluffy.
- Beat the eggs into the butter mixture one at a time until you have a smooth, creamy batter.
- Enhance the flavor by adding freshly squeezed lemon juice and finely grated lemon zest, then stir until fully incorporated.
- Mix flour and milk into the butter mixture slowly to make a smooth batter. Beat the mixture until everything is combined and lump-free.
- Grease a loaf pan that fits snugly inside your air fryer basket and carefully pour in the batter.
- Air-fried the loaf pan for 45 minutes.
- If a toothpick inserted in the center comes out clean, the food is ready to be served. This cooking method ensures an even bake and a perfectly cooked loaf.
- After everything is done, take the loaf pan out of the air fryer and leave it to cool for ten minutes.
- Serve the cake warm

Variations:

- For added tangy flavor, drizzle powdered sugar, lemon juice, and lemon zest over the lemon pound cake.
- Add blueberries, raspberries, or any other fruit for a delicious lemon pound cake.

Air Fryer Chocolate Fondue:

- Preparation time: 5 minutes
- Cooking time: 10 minutes
- Servings: 4

Nutrition facts (per serving): 294 Cal (21g fat, 3g protein, 3g fiber)

Ingredients:

- Semi-sweet chocolate chips: 1 cup
- Heavy cream: 1/2 cup
- Vanilla extract: 1/2 tsp
- Pinch of salt
- Assorted dipping items (e.g., strawberries, bananas, pound cake, pretzels)

Instructions:

- Pre-heat the air fryer at 350°F (175°C) for 5 minutes.
- Mix chocolate chips, heavy cream, vanilla extract, and salt in a microwave-safe bowl.
- Microwave the mixture for 1-2 minutes, stirring every 30 seconds, until the chocolate fully melts and the mixture is smooth.

- Pour the chocolate mixture into a heat-safe bowl or fondue pot in the air fryer basket.
- Place the bowl or pot into the air fryer basket and cook for 5-7 minutes, occasionally stirring, until the chocolate is warm and slightly bubbly.
- Serve the warm chocolate fondue with your favorite dipping items.

Variations:

- Instead of semi-sweet chocolate chips, use dark chocolate chips.
- Instead of semi-sweet, use white chocolate chips without vanilla.
- Before melting chocolate, add a pinch of cinnamon, nutmeg, or cayenne.
- Stir chopped nuts (such as almonds, hazelnuts, or peanuts) into the warm chocolate fondue before serving.

Air Fryer Vanilla Bean Crème Brûlée

- Prep Time: 10 minutes
- Cook Time: 25-30 minutes
- Serves: 4

Nutrition facts (per serving): 442 Cal (35g fat, 5g protein, 0g fiber)

Ingredients:

- Heavy cream: 1 and 1/2 cups
- Granulated sugar: 1/2 cup
- Egg yolks: 4
- Vanilla bean, split lengthwise and scraped
- Additional granulated sugar for topping

Instructions:

- Put the air fryer into preheating mode and set the temperature to 320°F (160°C) for 5 minutes.
- Pour heavy cream into a medium saucepan and add a vanilla bean (including the scraped seeds) to prepare the cream mixture. Heat the mixture over medium heat until it comes to a simmer. Once it reaches the simmering point, remove the saucepan from heat and allow the mixture to steep for 10 minutes, allowing the vanilla bean to infuse its flavor into the cream.

- Whisk the egg yolks and 1/2 cup granulated sugar in a separate mixing bowl until light and fluffy.
- Gradually whisk the hot cream mixture into the egg mixture, stirring constantly.
- Strain the mixture through a fine-mesh sieve into a measuring cup or bowl with a spout to remove any bits of vanilla bean or egg solids.
- Evenly distribute the mixture into four ramekins. After that, place them inside the air fryer basket.
- Bake the custard for 25-30 minutes until it is fully set with a slight jiggle in the center.
- Let the ramekins cool to room temperature before refrigerating for at least 2 hours.
- When ready to serve, sprinkle a thin layer of granulated sugar over each crème brûlée and use a kitchen torch to caramelize the sugar until it is golden brown and bubbly.
- Serve after cooling.

Variations:

- Substitute the vanilla bean with other flavorings like coffee, almond extract, or citrus zest for a different twist on classic crème brûlée.
- Top with fresh fruit or whipped cream for added flavor and texture.

Air Fryer Blackberry Hand Pies:

- Prep time: 15 minutes
- Cook time: 12 minutes
- Servings: 4

Nutrition facts (per serving): 237 Cal (11g fat, 2g protein, 2g fiber)

Ingredients:

- Fresh blackberries: 1 cup
- Granulated sugar: 1/4 cup
- Cornstarch: 1 tablespoon
- Vanilla extract: 1/2 teaspoon
- Refrigerated pie crust, thawed: 1 sheet
- Egg: 1
- Water: 1 tablespoon
- Coarse sugar: 1 tablespoon

Instructions:

- Preheat the air fryer to 375°F (190°C) for 5 minutes.

- Mix gently blackberries, sugar, cornstarch, and vanilla in a medium bowl.

- On a surface dusted with flour, roll out the pie crust and cut it into four rectangles of similar size.

- Place a scoop of the blackberry mixture on one side of each rectangle, leaving a thin border around the edge.
- After placing the filling in the center of the dough, bring the remaining half of the dough over it and crimp the sides with a fork to seal it.
- Mix water and eggs in a small bowl.
- Apply the egg wash to the surface of the pies using a brush, ensuring complete coverage. Then, generously sprinkle coarse sugar on top of the egg wash to add a delightful crunch and sweetness to the finished product.
- Put the hand pies in the air fryer's basket, ensuring they do not contact one another.
- Fry in the air for 10 to 12 minutes or until golden brown and crisp.
- Before serving, let the hand pies cool for a few minutes.

Variations:

- Choose raspberries or blueberries instead of blackberries.
- Add nutmeg or cinnamon to the blackberry filling for taste.
- Serve hand pies with vanilla ice cream.

Air Fryer Salted Caramel Popovers:

- Preparation time: 15 minutes
- Cooking time: 20 minutes
- **Serving size: 4**

Nutrition facts (per serving): 337 Cal (11g fat, 8g protein, 1g fiber)

Ingredients:

- All-purpose flour: 1 cup
- Salt: 1/2 teaspoon
- Granulated sugar: 2 tablespoons
- Large eggs: 2
- Milk: 1 cup
- Unsalted butter, melted: 1 tablespoon
- Vanilla extract: 1 teaspoon

- Salted caramel sauce: 1/2 cup
- Confectioners' sugar for dusting

Instructions:

- Whisk the granulated sugar, salt, and flour in a mixing bowl until well combined.
- Mix egg whites, milk, melted butter, vanilla essence, and vanilla bean in a separate bowl.
- Mix both the liquid and the dry components. Mixed until smooth.
- Put the air fryer into preheating mode and set the temperature to 350°F (175°C) for 5 minutes.
- Coat your muffin tin with a thin layer of non-stick cooking spray to prevent your muffins from sticking.
- Pour enough batter into each muffin cup to fill it about 3/4 Full.
- Cook the muffin pan in the air fryer basket for 20 minutes until the golden brown popovers rise.
- Take the muffin tray from the air fryer and allow the popovers to cool for a few minutes.

- Before serving, drizzle some salted caramel sauce over each popover and sprinkle some confectioners' sugar on top.

Variations:

- Remove the sugar and vanilla essence from the batter for a savory variant, and add herbs, cheese, or fried bacon pieces.
- Instead of salted caramel sauce, consider honey, chocolate sauce, or fruit compote.

Air Fryer Cinnamon Bun Twists

- Preparation Time: 15 minutes
- Cooking Time: 10-12 minutes
- Servings: 4

Nutrition facts (per serving): 257 Cal (15g fat, 2g protein, 1g fiber)

Ingredients:

- Puff pastry, thawed: 1 sheet
- Unsalted butter, melted: 2 tablespoons
- Granulated sugar: 2 tablespoons
- Ground cinnamon: 1 tablespoon
- Powdered sugar: 1/4 cup

- Milk: 1 tablespoon
- Vanilla extract: 1/4 teaspoon

Instructions:

- Put the air fryer into preheating mode and set the temperature to 375°F (190°C) for 5 minutes.
- Unfold the puff pastry and brush with melted butter.
- Add some ground cinnamon and granulated sugar to the greased pastry sheet.
- To begin, fold the pastry sheet in half and gently press the edges together to create a seal.
- Next, using either a sharp knife or a pizza cutter, cut the pastry sheet into strips that are approximately one inch wide.
- Place each pastry strip in the air fryer basket after twisting it a few times.
- Cook the cinnamon bun twists in an air fryer for ten to twelve minutes, until they are golden brown and puffy.
- Make a smooth glaze by mixing powdered sugar, milk, and vanilla essence in a small bowl.

- Drizzle glaze over warm cinnamon bun twists.
- Enjoy your delicious Air Fryer Cinnamon Bun Twists!

Variations:

- Add chopped dried fruit like apricots, raisins, or cranberries to the cinnamon sugar mixture for a fruity twist.
- For a nutty twist, sprinkle chopped almonds, pecans, or walnuts on the pastry sheet before folding it in half.

Air Fryer Monkey Bread

- Prep Time: 10 minutes
- Cook Time: 20 minutes
- Total Time: 30 minutes
- Servings: 6

Nutrition facts (per serving): 349 Cal (14g fat, 3g protein, 1g fiber)

Ingredients:

For the bread

- Rhodes White Dinner Rolls (or any pre-made frozen dough), thawed to room temperature: 12
- Brown sugar: 1/2 cup
- Ground cinnamon: 1 teaspoon
- Unsalted butter, melted: 4 tablespoons

For the glaze:

- Powdered sugar: 1/2 cup
- Milk (1-2 tablespoons, depending on desired consistency): 1-2 tablespoons
- Pure vanilla extract: 1/2 teaspoon

Instructions:

- In a bowl, brown sugar and cinnamon were stirred until combined.
- One-half of a stick of butter was melted in a separate bowl.
- Brush the inside of an air fryer-safe pan with melted butter. Make sure the pan fits your air fryer.
- After your frozen rolls defrost to room temperature, divide them in half, roll each piece in butter, dredge in the sugar mixture, and place them in the pan.
- When you have finished placing all your rolls into the pan, sprinkle any leftover butter and sugar over the top.
- Put the air fryer into preheating mode and set the temperature to 390°F (195°C) for 5 minutes.
- Afterward, turn off the air fryer and place the monkey bread pan inside. Allow the bread to sit and rise for approximately 30 minutes.

- Cover your pan with foil after the monkey bread has risen to prevent the air fryer's heating element from burning.
- Set the air fryer at 340°F (170 °C) and cook for 10–15 minutes. After 10 minutes, check with an instant-read thermometer. Bread is ready when it reaches 185 °C (85 °C.)
- Mix powdered sugar, vanilla, and milk until slightly runny to make the glaze.
- Remove the foil and bake for 3–4 minutes to gently brown the top. Remove the pan from the oven with caution.
- Wait a few minutes for the pan to cool, invert a plate over it, and then flip the pan onto the platter.
- Add glaze and enjoy.

Air Fryer Dessert Recipes

Did you enjoy this book?

I want to thank you for purchasing and reading this book. I hope you get a lot out of it.

Can I ask a quick favor, though?

If you enjoyed this book, I would appreciate it if you could leave me a positive review on Amazon.

I love getting feedback from my customers, and reviews on Amazon do make a difference. I read all my reviews and would appreciate your thoughts.

Thanks so much.

April Kelsey

P.s. You can click here to go directly to the book on Amazon and leave your review.

DISCLAIMER

This Air Fryer Dessert recipe is written as a purely informational and educational resource. It is not intended to be medical advice or a medical guide.

Although proper care has been taken to ensure the validity and reliability of the information provided in this book, readers are advised to exercise caution before using any information, suggestions, or methods described.

The writer does not advocate using any of the suggestions, diets, or health programs mentioned in this book. This book does not intend to replace a medical professional, a doctor, or a physician. The information in this book should not be used without explicit advice from medically trained professionals, especially in cases where urgent diagnosis and medical treatment are needed.

The author or publisher cannot be held responsible for any personal or commercial damage caused by misinterpreting or misunderstanding any part of the book.

Printed in Great Britain
by Amazon